MISSISSIPPI MEETS MINNESOTA

The Three-Strand Cord of Spurgeon and Deb

Deborah Tronnes Wiggins

Copyright @ 2022 Deborah Tronnes Wiggins

All rights reserved. No part of this publication may be reproduced or transmitted in any form or by any electronic or mechanical means including photo copying, recording, or any information storage and retrieval system now known or to be invented, without permission in writing from the publisher or the author.

Scripture quotations marked KJV are from the Holy Bible, King James Version. The KJV is in public domain.

All Scripture quotations, unless otherwise indicated, are taken from the Holy Bible, New International Version®, NIV®. Copyright ©1973, 1978, 1984, 2011 by Biblica, Inc.™ Used by permission of Zondervan. All rights reserved worldwide. www.zondervan.comThe "NIV" and "New International Version" are trademarks registered in the United States Patent and Trademark Office by Biblica, Inc.™

Scripture quotations marked ESV are from the Holy Bible, English Standard Version, copyright © 2001 by Crossway Bibles, a publishing ministry of Good News Publishers. Used by permission. All rights reserved.

The Holy Bible, Berean Study Bible, BSB. Copyright ©2016, 2020 by Bible Hub. Used by Permission. All Rights Reserved Worldwide.

Scripture quotations marked (GNT) are from the Good News Translation in Today's English Version- Second Edition Copyright © 1992 by American Bible Society. Used by Permission.

Scripture quotations marked (NLT) are taken from the Holy Bible, New Living Translation, copyright ©1996, 2004, 2015 by Tyndale House Foundation. Used by permission of Tyndale House Publishers, Carol Stream, Illinois 60188. All rights reserved.

Scripture quotations marked BLB are from the Blue Letter Bible.

Cover Designer: Robin Black

Name: Deborah Tronnes Wiggins
Title: Mississippi Meets Minnesota: The Three-Strand Cord of Spurgeon and Deb/ By Deborah Tronnes Wiggins
ISBN: paperback 978-1-953114-95-2
     e-book 978-1-953114-94-5
LCCN: 2022913605

Subjects: 1. Books/Christian Books & Bibles/Romance
2. Books/Biographies & Memoirs/Specific Groups/Marriage
3. Books/Self-Help/Personal Transformation

Published by EA Books Publishing, a division of
Living Parables of Central Florida, Inc. a 501c3
EABooksPublishing.com

Forward

The words Deborah has written literally vaulted off the pages as time-etched images paraded across my mind...page after page...

- I could hear the intensity of their conversations.
- I could see the smile creep onto the edges of Spurgeon's lips and as he expressed his intense love for his bride.
- I could feel the warmth and love exude from their hearts as story after story communicated unadulterated love and acceptance.

That summer night so many years ago when I, as young pastor, met Mississippi (Spurg) and Minnesota (Deb) and was invited into that love and acceptance will never be forgotten.
   The trajectory of my life changed.
      ...The way I viewed ethnic differences was transformed.
         ...The mode of how Biblical, martial love is communicated was solidified again and again in my heart and mind.

The words on the pages of this book are so much more than words. They are a crystal-clear revelation of how a Mississippian and a Minnesotan can meet, fall in love, and fully live the life that God designed for them; filled with passion and purpose. It exemplifies the fulfillment of the prayer that Jesus prayed, that life on earth might clearly reflect the realities of heaven.

Sam Todd
Lead Pastor
G3 Church

Table of Contents

Chapter 1: Meet and Greet 1

Chapter 2: I'll Do Me 4

Chapter 3: Getting to Know All About You 23

Chapter 4: Settling In 34

Chapter 5: The Interracial Climate of the Early 1980s 42

Chapter 6: Seeking the Plan Together 55

Chapter 7: Living the Dream 60

Chapter 8: Learning to be Country Again 66

Chapter 9: Those Are Some Fascinating ISMS! 76

Chapter 10: And All That Jazz 85

Chapter 11: Emotional Intelligence Trumps 91

Chapter 12: It Can't Be Just All Roses 103

Chapter 13: Party Place 111

Chapter 14: Healthy Busy 119

Chapter 15: Turning 90 123

Chapter 16: In Weakness There is Strength 127

Chapter 17: Interactive Fun Stuff 139

About the Author 149

Dedication

Uncle Al (Alvin Tronnes) embraced me with a pure and warm love.

Auntie Marna (Ambhuel) prayed for me consistently.

To them, I owe a lifetime of gratitude.

CHAPTER 1

Meet and Greet

THE FASCINATING ASPECT of loneliness over a decade of time is that it actually begins working in your favor. You can depend on loneliness to be present, easily identified, and consistent. You can even use it as an excuse, mimicking countless other gatherings where you either don't go, or you leave early. You tell others that you need that alone time. Disengaging is the perfect behavior if you don't want someone to want you, and you don't want to want someone.

And all those wonderful survival tactics work superbly, until the day the one your soul loves captures your every thought and threatens to break your long-standing friendship with loneliness.

How did I dare know that this man was undeniably going to threaten my way of life? Because I had met him twelve years earlier and was smitten with his charm, dignity, and smile. We met in the Windy City where we both worked for the board of education. As the fireman at Hartigan Elementary School, Spurgeon Wiggins Jr. was responsible for heating and cooling the building and frequently greeted our carpool of four women teachers when we entered the boiler room through the rear parking lot. His prize-winning face and warm greetings soon won him the title of "The Black Robert Redford of Hartigan School." It was the early '70s, Redford was the rage, and this was meant to be a true compliment. Today we would rightfully say, "The Denzel Washington of Hartigan School." So, pick your handsome!

The first time Spurgeon and I engaged in a conversation was at the payphone booth outside the principal's office. I waited out his lengthy stay in the cubical because I needed to make a call. Sliding the phone booth door open (how things have changed!), he apologized for my long wait, saying he had to speak with all three of his teenaged girls each morning so they wouldn't have any excuse not to get up and out for school. That was impressive.

But, alas, there was a fatal flaw in our meeting and in my magnetic attraction to the man. I was married to another man, and he was married to another woman. And so, we passed our pleasantries on work days and enjoyed a healthy social life with coworkers on some weekends.

After a year or so of greetings at the boiler room door and telephone booth, Spurgeon and I started eating lunch together in my classroom some days. We then gravitated to looking forward, daily, to our sharing.

Walking in that classroom door, he was no doubt eye-candy. His sense of dignity and propriety displayed itself with each step forward. But it was his inner light that preceded him. There was an aura about him. His warmth encompassed me. His purity drew me. His rich, deep skin and resonating voice swallowed me. His attentiveness made me feel valued. He valued what came out of my mouth. What I said mattered to him. I mattered to him. I wished someone at home would send me the same message.

The noon break was getting to be indispensable for my wellbeing. I sensed it was the same for him. Oddly enough, just talking with one another, about nothing and everything, helped us de-stress from our challenged marriages and our jobs.

But it is *never* a good idea to share daily joys and pains with someone who is not your spouse. We discussed stopping the lunch gig. We agreed that our friendship was unhealthy to our marriages. He wisely upped for a promotion in another school.

His moving to a new job helped, but we still engaged in a call or a meet-and-greet at a party of mutual friends. Each time I saw him I wanted to follow him. Anywhere.

Then the time came, five years after I met this dynamic man, that I could no longer be *anywhere* near him. Plain and simple, I thought he was everything that a man should be, and, ashamedly, I was enraptured. So, I chose the best action possible and took a job 1,200 miles away in Houston, Texas and moved with my husband. I believed an insurmountable distance would make it possible for me to forget about that fine specimen of a man.

CHAPTER 2

I'll Do Me

THOUGH MOVING TO THE Lone Star State was a positive move in a variety of ways, it was not the fixer upper that I had hoped for in regard to our marriage. My hopes were to concentrate on bettering our relationship and to get him to focus some attention on me. I was lonely. I had been lonely with him our whole marriage.

The worst thing about that was that I pretty much deserved to be miserable. I'd married a Peruvian man at the drop of a hat for all the wrong reasons. He proposed shortly after our initial meeting, and I was afraid I would die before I had another chance to get married and have an intimate relationship. So, I said yes.

Quite the idiotic mentality, for certain. But that idiotic thought doesn't look quite as puzzling if one knows a bit of my background. Any "normal" person would be aghast at that mentality and would wonder why a person of reasonable intellect would stoop to such behavior. In my heart and mistaken thinking, I believed I would follow in the short-lived footsteps of my biological Mother, Dorothy, who died at 28, leaving behind three children and a loving husband. My father, Roy Tronnes, a WW II Purple Heart recipient, died of gases thrown in ditches during the war. He passed away less than a year after our mom, leaving three orphans behind.

My father's brother, Emil, promised his dying sibling that he and his wife, Hildur, would see that we were placed with family. They initially took all of us in, adding to their own three sons for a total of six kids. But alas, half a dozen kids, suddenly, became undoable. Shortly after the adoptions, my bio brothers and I were separated. They went to Northern Minnesota to live with another uncle, and I stayed at my new home with three new brothers and two new parents.

There's not much I can tell about those early years after adoption because trauma overcame me and robbed me of my memory. They say that at three years old I could count to ten and tie my shoes. Months after my fourth birthday, I could do neither of those tasks. My young school life faltered, and I transformed to being dumb as a doornail for years. I have true empathy for kids who live in shock and find academics difficult and life confusing. It takes years to grow out of post-traumatic stress disorder. Time and God seemed to be the only help. Who knew anything of such matters back in the 1950s?

My three new brothers treated me like any sister. They were my playmates. They were kind, comforting, and taunting, just like all brothers.

Our parents were afflicted with a couple of garden varieties of maladies. But, they both worked hard, were well read, and taught all of us a tremendous sense of work ethics and responsibility. We grew up with those drawbacks and pluses for the duration of our formative years.

My ultimate healing came from an early relationship with the Lord and a fresh spring creek that meandered throughout our neighborhood. Kids of all ages in our East Old Shakopee Road neighborhood spent hours, and even days, tromping the forest that surrounded the creek. We would follow the stream for a mile or so, pass by a waterfall area constructed by the Civilian Conservation Corps, and ultimately came to the Minnesota River and Bass Pond. There we idled time away with wading, catching minnows, throwing rocks, finding sea glass, sliding off of the miniature waterfall wall, swinging on grape vines, and cooking apples stuffed with cinnamon and sugar over an open fire.

I frequently explored the creek with or without the company of others.

In the winter, the same streamed area turned into a white wonderland for sledding and tobogganing. All the ills of life disappeared for you in the time you sledded. Adrenalin ran high. And if you built a jump that was massively too high for you to go over safely, then you had a legitimate reason to cry icicle tears. I think it all built strong bones, good health, and character.

The creek and its setting set the foundation for my lifelong sense of adventure. My biological mother, Dorothy, was mostly Norwegian and some Bohemian. Her siblings told me she was a free spirit. I've often thought it interesting that she passed that on to me.

I'm sure the childhood trauma had passed by the time I was a young adult, but that left-over residue of insecurity stood tall and strong when it came to my picking a mate.

I had not taken the time to know my fiancé and fall in love with him. I wanted to get married and have a family before I turned twenty-four, because I felt that an early death would be my eminent fate also, just like my parents. And there was some validity to my fear of an early demise. My bio Mom died of liver malfunctions and my liver is also compromised. I have used massive quantities of herbs, essential oils and liver cleansers over my lifetime to sustain a functioning liver.

As a result of the false belief that I would die young (I am 73 years old as I write this memoir), I rashly asked God if this man was "the one." But, in reality, I didn't care what God answered, nor what He really wanted for me because I was desperate. Or so I felt!

So, in that desperation, I married a man with erratic behavior who seemed to prize his *paisanos* (countrymen) far above our relationship. He worked sparsely, yet felt comfortable, having moved several of his countrymen into our tiny apartment. I was to hold down the ship. My likes or dislikes, feelings, and desires, were inconsequential to this man. As a young, cute bride I felt I deserved some attention. I worked hard to win his sparse acknowledgment. This was to no avail.

My heart sometimes slipped into comforting thoughts of Spurgeon Wiggins in Chicago. I never had to beg him to hear me. He thought I was quite captivating.

But, oh well! Who cares? I had made my bed and now I was sleeping in it! I vowed that if I ever made a marriage bed again, I would be more selective about my bedfellow.

In Houston, I worked as an education specialist with the housing authority to help reduce crime in the units. I liked the job but couldn't handle the never-ending heat of the city.

We moved to San Francisco.

Why did we move? Mostly because we could. At this point, I had caught on to the thrill of moving and travel. My husband had friends on the West Coast, and they invited us to come and stay with them. That was enough.

Between waitressing, my little B.A. in education, and my relatively affable personality, I saw that I could easily obtain a stable income anywhere I went. Plus, I was never afraid of hard work or new situations and actually relished the newness of all the travel. In San Francisco, I waitressed in several great family restaurants.

I like waitressing. I like when people come in all "hangry" and I serve them a great meal expediently with a smile. They turn from lions into lambs. It's fun to see people satisfied and happy.

San Francisco was a short-lived stay, though his Peruvian friends that we lived with were quite beautiful. In that time, I allowed myself to be persuaded to take my pension and savings and fly to Peru, his native country, to live. And we did it!

Eh. I was adventuresome. I was game!

Peru, South America, in the early '80s was a dangerous place. The revolutionary group, *Sendero Luminoso,* the Shining Path, was terrorizing the country, killing and maiming throughout the land. They particularly did not like North Americans or missionaries.

Once, in Lima, on an empty street downtown during siesta, I had rocks thrown at me. In Arricucho, a resident hit my visiting Wisconsin girlfriend with brass knuckles while passing on the sidewalk.

But, in the big picture, God guarded my life through numerous dangers because He had a plan for me after Peru. And in the meantime, while living and traveling in this Andes Mountain region of the world, I gained a beautiful second culture and second language.

There is a tidy mountain town in Peru called Huancayo. It is a gathering place for the many artisans on weekends. The Natives of the area trek their weavings, baskets, *mates* (a carved and painted or burned gourd), llama and alpaca sweaters, and all manner of artistry to this town's central plaza. Often, big artisan stores in Lima, the capital, 120 miles away, travel to this mountain retreat to buy truckloads of product to sell in the big cities. If you go with a skilled barterer, you can walk away with some great prices on outrageously stunning art. If you are fortunate, you can snag an Incan weaving that may be found in many forms, whether clothing, wall art, or rugs.

My husband said we could go there, and he would barter on my behalf. It takes a native Peruvian to barter with the venders. Not just because of the language, but because of the evolved art of bartering.

When you are in an artisan market where they are *known* to barter, the act of vending turns into a spectator sport! At first, you think the discourse is escalating toward an argument when the volume rises, and body language begins speaking. Ultimately, the two contestants start laughing at themselves and their bantering skills! It is amusing and astonishing for an American who is accustomed to walking into stores with established prices.

But the adventure to that mountain art paradise was cancelled by my Peruvian husband. He was sporting one of his giant attitudes and didn't feel in the mood to go, so he scratched the bus trip to Huancayo.

Sometimes, God uses even selfish people to further his plans. That very bus full of people went over the side of the Andes with no survivors.

For whatever combination of reasons, my other half acted as if he barely knew me while living in his home country. He hooked up with his old neighborhood and university friends and all but forgot that I was living there as his mate. It was uncanny how very much time he spent out in the streets. I wondered about the mixed company he kept.

It did little good to ask questions or discuss the matter, because he just stared at me and didn't respond. Not a word. I fell deeper into that lonely pit.

It turned out nontheless fascinating to see life through a different lens for those two years. I ended up going to the American church in Lima to meet friends, so I had someone to hang with.

And hang we did! I ended up working and traveling with Paul and Marty, life-long missionaries. He is Brit; she, North American. While working for the two-century old Scripture Union, or *Union Biblica,* they ran camps, schools for the deaf, and orphanages throughout the country. I worked with this dynamic couple, volunteering for vacation Bible school, and they quickly nabbed me as a resource for their passions. We worked together nearly two years and set the stage for future interaction.

One of the quirky things I did in my life was memorize things I found fascinating. I recovered from my brain trauma by fifth grade, after which I caught up on my sorry academic life. I found memorization a task that intrigued me. I was introduced to Longfellow's *Hiawatha's Song* and memorized the first five stanzas, because I loved the forest and living near water.

Romans chapter 12 (KJV) was relatively easy to learn as well as helpful to my behavior. I particularly needed to remind myself to "bless them which persecute you. Bless them and curse not" (verse 14). It helped my empathetic character to be reminded to: "Rejoice with those who do rejoice and weep with those who weep" (verse 15). This would work well with my God-given strength of compassion and my desire to serve God by serving others.

And when Shel Silverstein's poetry came out, what self-respecting, young-at-heart person did not memorize the hilarious "Boa Constrictor" or "There's Too Many Kids in the Tub?" They are so much fun said aloud.

While living in Peru, a native friend challenged me to memorize the poetic names of the 14 Imperial Incas.

Each of the names falls on my ears like a melody. And here they are, for your pleasure.

Manco Capac

Sinchi Roca

LLoque Yupanqui

Mayta Capac

Capac Yupanqui

Inca Roca

Yahuar Huaca

Huiracocha

Pachacutec

Amaru Inca Yupanqui

Tupac Yupanqui

Huayna Capac

Huascar

Atahualpa

Seeing them in print may do nothing for you, but if you hear them, they sound like poetry.

Though the magnetism of the handsome face of Atahualpa is alluring, it is actually the ninth Imperial, Pachacutec, who intrigues me. I fell in like with him when my friend told us all about this powerful, colorful, well-rounded character.

History tells us that Pachacutec expanded the Inca Empire tremendously. He improved the architectural plan of Cusco, their capital city, and the famed Machu Picchu, thought to be a religious center, was built on his behalf.

A substantial aspect of Pachacutec's life is the spiritual. And since history everywhere has the habit of excluding spiritual happenings, our Peruvian Paul told us that his research into this Imperial's life led him to the following bit of fascinating information.

Like many cultures around the world, even today, leaders are sometimes considered to be gods. (Caesar, in Rome, was told he was god, and he believed it.)

But Pachacutec resisted that idea and went on a pilgrimage with his entourage to explore another philosophy. He and troupe went on a forty-day journey to Puno, Peru.

You likely remember Puno from your high school geography as the city nearest Lake Titicaca, the highest elevated lake in the world. I was told this has become a spiritual center of attention worldwide.

In Puno, when Pachacutec told his entourage that he was, indeed, not god, they asked him how he came to such a sacrilegious thought.

"We have been here for many days now. You say that I am the sun and god. But every day as I awaken, the light is coming up in the east, same place, same time. Someone orders that sun, and it is not me!"

"Well then, who does order the sun?" The entourage needed to know.

"It is the one who made the sun and moon and stars," stated the profound Inca Imperial.

"So, we can call him Creator!"

"No. Creator limits him," opined the ruler. It confines him to one dimension and leaves him there. He is far more than just the creator."

"So, what do we call him?" His followers were desperate to know.

"Call him, '*He Is*,'" answered Pachacutec, reverently.

He Is?

This is my portrayal of Atahualpa, the last Imperial Inca. It is a published piece through Sommerset Studio. The face was extracted from a decades old Lima, Peru, newspaper article that was embellished with embossing and other methods.

Wow, really? That is the same name God told for Moses to use (for Him) when the Israelites asked about God's name after He met Moses on Mount Sinai. God said tell them "I Am." And here is a man who never read the Word but searched for God with all his "heart and soul and strength," (Deuteronomy 6:5, paraphrased.) just as scripture says, and he found the great "I Am!"

That is profound.

Despite the wonderful history that I learned in Peru, the immediate marriage history continued on a downhill slide. Ultimately, I divorced the man I had no business marrying in the first place. I divorced him not because he hurt me, but because he kept on hurting me.

My suspicion is, in retrospect, that my Peruvian husband suffered with an undiagnosed case of bi-polar disorder. Having no familiarity with this disease, I did not recognize the illness and could handle it no longer. I returned to live in my home state of Minnesota. I'd been lonely in that poor marriage for nine years and was convinced that returning to my roots and nature would be my healer and friend. This was the perfect place to continue the lonely stretch of my life.

Oh, what relief! And how sad it was that pain was not my primary emotion. I spent nine years married to a man, and when it was all over, relief topped the list of feelings! That is lamentable.

My brother picked me up in his snappy car/truck to take me to his little retreat in the woods in the northern part of the state. En route home, well after dusk, a large furry animal dashed in front of his car/truck and continued crossing the road.

"Was that what I think it was!" I blurted.

"If you are thinking that it was a timber wolf, you would be right," answered brother Roy.

The stunning wolf's back was nearly the height of the hood of the car/truck, and he looked like a giant, gorgeous German shepherd. The remote setting and the wonderful wolf convicted me of what I already knew: This was the right place for me right then.

I related to this lone wolf. Was he kicked out of the pack, or did he choose to leave to avoid conflict and pain? Was he hurt? Did he cry? Would we hear him at night? Only distance and vastness of the dense forest would muffle that sound. Would he make it all alone in the dark?

Either way, he was a determined creature, taking a solo flight into the night. Ahhh, my kin, the wolf. He'd find a place for his size-large personality in another part of the forest.

People that didn't know me well warned me that I couldn't run away from my problems. Running away, I was not. And anyway, that doesn't work. Jonah proved that. I felt like I was getting a raccoon off my back. Maybe the wolf was getting a coon off its back also. I read that, when initiating a battle, the masked bandits jump on the backs of canines and immediately reach around to scratch their eyeballs out.

Removing oneself from abuse, neglect, and painful attacks is not running away.

Besides, I had put out a fleece with God in regard to leaving my first marriage (Judges 6: 33-40). I adopted Gideon's remarkable request toward God when he was indecisive about whether to attack the Mideonites or not. He asked God to answer his dilemma by responding to a test. He would sleep on the threshing floor. Next to him, on the floor, he put out a sheepskin. If the sheepskin was wet in the morning while the threshing floor was dry, it was meant for the Israelites to fight. The next morning, Gideon had to wring out the wet fleece, but the floor was bone dry. Wanting to be positive he had it right, he asked God to do just the reverse the next night. When Gideon awoke on the threshing floor the second morning, the floor was wet, and the fleece was dry. That response signified God's answer to the Gideon's dilemma. God would be with them in victory over the Mideonites.

I was back in San Francisco. I had flown from Peru to the Bay Area, alone, because my husband reportedly had matters to wind up in Peru after our two-year stint. I went ahead to procure apartment, job, vehicle, and phone. He returned at his leisure while I held down the fort with another lucrative waitress job.

On his return he set me up for yet another string of difficulties, some dangerous, again. Nothing was ever easy with this man. With all the stress and neglect, I started crying three and four hours a day. That had never happened before, nor has it happened since. It scared me. For the first time in my life, I suspected I was close to a mental breakdown.

It is not that I whimpered into my pillow, feeling sorry for myself. No, I mean full blown, out loud, wrenching cries where I needed pillows to muffle the raging despair. I lived in a two-flat and didn't want others to hear me wail.

Praying for a plan, I was led to Gideon's practice: A fleece test for God. The Almighty comforted me to make this agreement with Him: I felt like my husband had proved time and again that he did not love me. But I was willing to accept the remote possibility that he did. (Oh, my goodness, we ladies are so pitiful. We just want to be loved, at all costs!)

So, God and I agreed: If my mate loved me, he would show unfettered kindness and love toward me in the next month. If he truly didn't love me, he would show it in a *grand* way and be even less caring.

Well, if God ever agrees to allow you a fleece, have no doubt that he will deal with you in no uncertain terms. This fleece was the real deal. It accomplished exactly what I'd asked.

During the next month, my ex did something so cold that I am embarrassed, to this day, that I had to live through that humiliation.

At this point, I ask the reader's forgiveness in leading you to a pinnacle without disclosing the details. The details mortified me then, and the thought of that negativity living on in written form does not make sense to me. Were it a cathartic telling, I would happily make the disclosure. But I cannot debase myself further by telling the details in print. No one's living nightmare should be outlined in detail. That would allow our misfortunes to define us, and that cannot happen.

Additionally, what kind of sensationalist would I be if I disclosed the cruel tale, and that became a prominent remembrance for the reader? That would mean that the Evil One had won.

Therefore, returning to the countryside of Northern Minnesota in my favorite environmental niche *was* cathartic. The first couple months I blared Gloria Gaynor's "I Will Survive" sporadically throughout the days. I bellowed with her, walking amongst the trees. I think she has helped oodles of women with that song.

The woods absorbed and drank my sorrows.

After the grief of failure diminished, I picked wild blueberries and played family ball games after church on Sundays. I watched eagles train their young to fly and smiled warmly as my new friends pointed out an otter family playing in the river. I learned to cross-country ski.

One Sunday morning in church, an astute business owner at the church I attended in Ball Club, Minnesota, asked if I would like a job telemarketing wild rice. Sales were outside of my expertise, but I was versatile, willing, and thrilled to be asked. Northern Minnesota had a tight job market at this point. I soon became acquainted with purchasing agents and chefs of fine restaurants all over the country.

New people, new skills. My days were filled with nature and peace. God was working.

My heart of laced vellum became strong enough to build on, like layers of a paper-mache project. Then the powerful medicine of nature, time and prayer began to salve my wounds, one layer at a time.

I suppose broken hearts come in varied forms, since we are all so different. Mine was fragile because of emotional neglect, stress, and cruelty. But I was confident that, given the right medicine, I would mend. That "word of God that is alive and active, and sharper than any two-edged sword." (Hebrews 4:12, NIV) would help me. Being away from all that mess and stress was like sanitizing an open wound. Cleaning out the dirt from the road rash of life is essential to wellness.

As an artist, I am firmly convicted that no one in America, poor or not, has to live in an ugly environment. My couple of years in the woods taught me to use the endless supply of environmental materials that were readily available to bring the intense beauty of the outdoors inside.

For a bit of needed side cash, I made and sold grapevine and pinecone wreaths. The Catholic church in town hired me to make a fifty-foot-long varied pine swag, which adorned the front of the church all Christmas season. I amassed feathers as well as paper birch and sent them as gifts to fellow artists who lived without these versatile medias. I even picked herbs (wild rose hips, Labrador leaves, and wintergreen leaves and berries in particular) and sold them to an herbal company that I contacted in Chicago.

My favorite hang buddies in Northern Minnesota, were a four-year-old named Lizzy, her 13- year-old brother, Mike, and her mom and dad. Since my brother's cabin was on the Daigle family's land, they opened their little hamlet to me, and we became fast friends.

The big girls, Di and I, donned cross-country skis and slid along for hours when it was five degrees above zero, but Lizzy and I enjoyed going on nature walks through her folks' woods. (Maybe I didn't enjoy her as much on my days off when Lizzy showed up at my door at 7:00 a.m.!) Her mother and father are an astute couple who raised their children to know a good deal about their woodsy environment. I'm no slouch myself in the area of wildflower knowledge, but Lizzy should have been on *Jeopardy* for woodsy growths. She sponged knowledge from her *Better Homes and Gardens* dad, Mike.

Lizzy

One day, while taking our customary woods walk to see what we could see, I spotted an unfamiliar flower. Knowing her "lifelong" training, I queried the four-year-old: "Do you know this flower, Lizzy?"

"Yes, that is an arbutus."

"Pretty. Thanks." We strolled on, eyes perusing flora and fauna. On return, we saw the flower again, and by that time I'd forgotten the name. Admitting same, I asked, again, for the flower's identity.

"Arbutus, Deb. 'R,' like the letter; 'bute,' as in beautiful; and 'us,' like you and me. Arbutus."

I never forgot. Now you won't either!

Trailing Arbutus

Lizzy's Dad, Mike, dropped by one afternoon with an invitation. "Deb, the wild blueberries are at their peak, if you'd like to pick. Just go over the garden fence and straight west into the woods, and you will find the clearing of berries."

Well, I was undeniably in the mood for fresh wild blueberries, so my dog, Sundown, and I went on the described hike. Finding the berry patch was a no-brainer. My nose led me there! I immediately got down on my haunches to pick and fill my bucket.

After about twenty minutes of great picking, I heard a rustling through the stillness of the woods. Thinking it was my dog, Sundown, who wandered off and was returning, I casually looked in the direction of the noise.

My eyes widened at the startling sight: A huge timber wolf, about thirty feet away, approached as he slunk through the foliage and prowled toward me. Down on my haunches, still, we glared at each other straight in the eyes as the gap narrowed. My brain suddenly remembered that you are *not* supposed to look a wild canine in the eyes because they perceive that as a challenge. I quickly diverted the stare.

At that moment, I thought that I might die.

The wolf skulked closer. Intent in his gaze, he increased his speed and pounced against my torso, knocking me over, along with the berry basket. He licked my face voraciously, took a mouthful of piled-up berries, slobbered half of them upon me as I lay, dazed, on the ground, and then trotted away!

No, that couldn't have happened!

Stunned on the woods floor, but unharmed, I tried to make sense of it all. Cautiously, I retrieved my pickings from the ground and returned home. Passing by Mike's house, I knocked on the open door and hollered for him. Still shaken, I hurried into the house and launched into the tale of the timber wolf licking my face!

Mike had the audacity to laugh!

"Mike, I almost died in your woods, and you are laughing! I don't find it funny in the least bit!"

"Deb, more than one-hundred years ago the state of Minnesota put up a $100 reward for anybody with concrete evidence that a timber wolf attacked a person. That money has never been claimed. What you saw was the neighbor's dog. The dog's mom was a German shepherd, she mated with a wolf, and he is the byproduct."

On future occasions, I met the dog in person. He was massive and could fool me any day as to his identity.

One stellar Saturday, with the pure air being the perfect baseball temperature, we had a neighborhood/family game in Mike's and Di's baseball field out north of the house. Grandmas and grandpas were there, some of them playing. Any child that could hold a bat could play. Men and women with rival baseball shirts and hats on threw barbs at each other.

The game was riotous. Toddlers played on a blanket in the sidelines and frequently squealed with delight. Adults that didn't play lined up their lawn chairs at good vantage points so they could jive the players. You'd have thought they'd brought bullhorns, given the hassle they gave the home-spun athletes.

Growing up with five brothers, I'd been a tomboy all my life and joined the boys on the diamond any day they let me. Even so, I was little better than a mediocre player. But that day I rocked on the field! I got on base every time and even hit in a few runs!

I wiped off the dandelion pollen, which kids had sprinkled on me at the post game celebration. Lizzy said it was fairy dust, and something magical was going to happen to me that night. It had already proven to be a fun and charming day.

After that stunning Northern Minnesota spring game, brother Roy and I sat on the couch at home talking about the great hits and snags in that game, when the phone rang.

We had just spent the afternoon and evening with nearly everybody we regularly hung out with, so we were not expecting anyone's call. Roy answered and, with a question on his face, extended the phone toward me.

"It's Spurgeon Wiggins . . . ?" he stated quizzically.

Spurgeon Wiggins Jr. was calling me? Why? It had been years since I had last seen him. Must be Lizzy's fairy dust.

Admittedly, I had thought about him over the years. I had thought about him a lot, since I left The Windy City in 1978 (this was 1984). But it was important to me to not think of him in a sinful manner. After all, I left Chicago primarily to vacate this man from my heart.

I had a rough but cozy hovel deep in the Northern woods of the Land of 17,000 Lakes (according to a study by the University of Minnesota Duluth). I had the mobility of a trusty truck and a job close to home that covered my needs. My creative life was burgeoning, while my social life was contentedly occupied. A good church and pastor kept me learning and growing. The environment encompassing our minute hamlet drew us all out to experience the immense beauty of the woodlands. Life had become quiet and unassuming.

So why was he calling me when I was doing so well?

He had acquired my address and number from a mutual friend.

We started writing. (Texting did not yet exist and my remote geographical spot would have made texting difficult, to this day.) The communications flowed and casual pages quickly turned into love letters.

The letters, from 700 miles away, didn't put the fear in me. They drew me closer to him as he revealed his sensitive side and bared his soul. He, too, had a final straw break the proverbial camel's back and ended his lengthy marriage. A continual widening gap in value systems put a strain on the relationship and ultimately drew him and his wife apart. Spurgeon said he had been going to leave for many years and finally walked out the door. He had wanted to see all three of his girls grown and out of the house, so he could ensure his brand of parental influence.

I did not feel threatened by his love until he asked me to return to Chicago and marry him. Then, oh my. My thoughts and heart reeled.

How could this be? I really had gotten into the groove of life as a contented, grown, capable woman who lived humbly in the dense woods of my home state.

And now Spurgeon Wiggins Jr. wanted me to return to Chicago and begin a new life with him?

Though the idea of engaging in a relationship with a man of Spurgeon's caliber was amazingly alluring, it was also threatening. I began having a kind of energy attack.

It felt like all the critters from *Where the Wild Things Are* were having a party in my head and tummy. It seemed like my insides were shouting. I had raucous days where all my energy exuded through my mouth and limbs.

This type of anxiety happens to me only when good excitement enters my life. I went for a walk in the woods and vocalized. I bellowed poetry and my favorite Bible verses. I conversed with the animals and plants. I said goodbye to the flora that I studied in the "Mushrooms and Other Wild Edibles" course I had taken at the local junior college from a man whom area people called, "The Euell Gibbons of Northern Minnesota." Goodbye fresh wintergreen berries with spongy red treats popping through the pure snow. Goodbye wild rose hips full of vitamin C. Goodbye lady slippers lining the forested, winding drive. Goodbye trailing arbutus and lovely Lizzy.

When the actual day came to leave Minnesota and drive my truck to Chicago, I was frightened out of my wits! My fright/flight syndrome drove me to radical thoughts. I had open-ended invitations from a couple of my business clientele who wanted very much to meet me in person. I could meet up with them and squelch the Windy City commitment.

Fear of failure, again, paralyzed me. God hates divorce. Micah 2:16.

I hate divorce. What if I failed, again?

No. Wrong thinking. What if we succeeded beyond measure? Love is a gift not to be ignored.

What if we had the marriage of the century?

Praying over that divorce syndrome and harebrained idea of going completely maverick, I chose to camp, solitary, on the shores of Lake Superior for two days instead.

It was July, and a cool mist from the deepest of the Great Lakes, Gitche Gumee (Ojibwa), shrouded the normal baby-blue summer sky with a gray sheath that extended from infinite height to the sand and pebbles of the beach. It was a suitable day to hunt for Lake Superior agates, as my Uncle Denny had taught all his girls and nieces and nephews to do. They have a stunning burnt orange hue and are prized amongst agate hunters. I was successful only regarding the "thrill of the hunt," so to speak. That was enough for me.

Superior has a shoreline that roars when the water is ruffled. On this momentous trip, I felt the undulating waves become a repetitive message of order and peace, order and peace, order and peace. Each moving ridge insisted on speaking resoundingly and affirmatively to me until I could decipher their strong, insistent message: "God does not give us the spirit of fear, but of courage and love and a sound mind" (2 Timothy 1:7, KJV).

Courage, love and a sound mind are precisely what I needed.

I read a lot of *The Word* those two days. Then I drove toward my wonderful destiny and the marvelous Spurgeon.

CHAPTER 3

Getting to Know All About You

DESPITE BEARING THE SAME name, Spurgeon Wiggins Jr. was both the antithesis of his father and an enigma to all. Beauty from the ashes, like raku ware.

God compares us all to clay numerous times in the Bible, molded by His hands into what He desires for each of us. Isaiah 45:9 (GNT) bears that out: "Does a *clay* pot dare argue with its *maker*, a pot that is like all the others? Does the clay ask the potter what he is doing? Does the pot complain that its maker has no skill?"

I have a bestie cousin, Julie, who owns a kiln and has excelled as a potter for decades. I likened Spurgeon to a piece of her raku-style pottery and asked her to describe for me the lengthy process of this stunning artistic achievement. Her response was detailed and experience-laden and far too-well expressed for me to change.

"God's creativity includes choosing from varieties of techniques, glazes, and firing processes," explained the potter, Julie. "And so, by His hands, we live our lives growing in Spirit (or not) and sharing what we contain with the other 'vessels' that God created.

"Being my brother in spirit, it is easy for me [cousin Julie is writing here] to see Spurgeon as likened to raku pottery, which is wonderfully unique in appearance with no two pieces alike. This is a result of the challenging building and firing methods.

"Although raku is not widely known as an art form, Spurgeon was noted for his rich looks and the metallic-like strength he possessed.

"Thus," continued the potter's description, "God took a huge piece of clay and molded it into an elegantly shaped vessel, which was to become Spurgeon Wiggins. It was quite sizable in order to hold the magnitude of Spurgeon's spirit, which became larger and larger as he grew from a child into a man. Consequently, working with this amount of clay is no easy task and can require revamping due to the challenges during the process. How true this is for Spurgeon's life as a boy from Mississippi who, grew into a *real* man who served his country and his large family throughout his eventful life. He faced the inherent formidability as an African American, experiencing prejudices that most cannot begin to comprehend. Unjust and grievous hardships persisted throughout his life. But God triumphed in building His illustrious Wiggins vessel.

"Continuing the prolonged art form," the potter proceeded, "the next step was the glaze, and God knew His choice would create a Spurgeon that would become a fabulously rich and colorfully dark (strong), metallic receptacle. One uses fire to bring a clay pot to maturity, God first built a special heat resistant box filled with all natural materials and which encompassed the vessel, and as such, buried to burn for hours. Thus, Spurgeon was infused with the Fire of Spirit until just at the right moment; God carefully lifted the red-hot vessel out of the kiln and plunged it into cold water.

"In this way Spurgeon emerged with that fine, crackled surface, representing the many insufferable trials and oppressions thrust upon him by the hands of racism. Yet his eyes still held the gaze of glazed fire, and his smooth dark skin betrayed the days of picking cotton in the hot sun. Through all, the laborious process and arduous journey, Spurgeon displayed the attainment of grace and dignity. His visage was a vessel of God."

The voice of experience continued: "God did not make many 'raku' pieces, yet these special vessels were scattered about the world for a special purpose of His design. Hence, Spurgeon is and was a quintessential human vessel, filled with God's love and accepting grace, a man-vase glazed with humble dignity, which he shared with all people who came into contact with him."

"Go, Cuz!" I say. I actually enjoyed inserting this uncensored script with another person's point of view on Spurgeon. This will help the reader know that my descriptions of dear Spurgie are authentic and not unrealistic on my part. This man stood out in a crowd!

Cuz continued, "Considering the life he was born into, raku is a felicitous analogy for Spurgeon Wiggins. Moreover, raku is one of few techniques that uses all four elements'—earth, air, fire, and water. In the Japanese culture the word 'raku' literally translates to, 'a happy accident.' How very fitting indeed for the debut of Spurgeon Wiggins Jr."

On the 6th of May 1930, Spurgeon Wiggins Jr. was born with skin the color of deep cinnamon, in the most segregated state in the Union—Mississippi. It was also the deepest part of the depression, and Mississippi held the title to not just being a poor state, it was the poorest. He was the second child of what would become ten siblings.

One may question why those in poverty would keep birthing babies, but it was a finely balanced equation of mouths to feed offset by many hands in the fields. After all, his folks were sharecroppers, the next level up from slavery. Having as many kids as possible ensured help with the sowing and the harvest. This became an unfortunate cross-cultural habit that perpetuated itself in many farming communities throughout the United States in our early history and into the twentieth century.

Permitted to attend school only on days that his folks didn't need him to pick cotton, Spurgeon was compliant and saddened, as he had a true yen for learning. On the days he was allowed to attend school, he had to walk five miles each way with his shoes around his neck because he wasn't supposed to wear them out. Each day, the school bus came to his neighborhood to pick up the White kids and sally them to school in comfort. Black children were abandoned by public-school transportation.

Food was scarce for the large family. His Dad frequently did migrant work and was gone for long spells of time. Spurgie said that many a day his mom would say, "Junior, go out and see if you can track a big turtle for dinner."

"Was that adventure fruitful?" I inquired curiously.

"Oh yes, most days I was blessed with finding dinner," he bragged, with a grin that lit his face.

"How do you distinguish the tracks of a turtle?" I asked, still intrigued. This was far from any dinner experience I ever had.

"Oh. Easily. They always drag their tail, so you see clawed prints that sort of shuffle along with a solid line through the middle," stated the tracker.

Determined to succeed in every area of his life, Spurgeon grew up quickly and moved north when he was eighteen and became a part of the huge, Great American Migration, when large percentages of African Americans left the agricultural South for the industrial North.

One of his paternal aunts had a three-flat brick building that she lived in and rented out. Spurgeon, as a favored nephew, set up a cot in her kitchen at night to sleep and folded it away during the day while he went to work. He performed chores for Auntie, to pay for room and board, so establishing himself in a new state.

After working in a Fig Newton cookie factory for two years, he was drafted into the army and became a munitions expert in the Korean War. He spent much of his time in 1951 and 1952 in Occupied Japan. Always one to advance himself, he completed his high school diploma while taking courses in Japanese.

But, of course, even after serving our country in war, he returned home to sit in the back of the bus in Chicago and all over his home country. Shame, shame on us.

With his army term completed, Spurgeon then returned to Chicago, married and started a family, and proceeded to bring, little by little, his whole birth family north. He made arrangements for each one of his eight siblings to also live in Chicago, the mecca of opportunity at the time.

A soldier more handsome I cannot imagine

In his adult life, Spurgeon strove relentlessly to educate himself in many forms, from his vocation of building trades to Spanish, basic mechanics, carpentry, calligraphy, Bible studies, building windmills, ballroom dancing, and more. He overcame his early, stifling education (as well as a hefty case of stuttering), to become a life-long learner, filled with wisdom.

Vocationally, Black Americans had to fight harder for good jobs, even in the '70s and '80s. The Chicago Board of Education hired Black males as custodians or firemen, but not as engineers, a more skilled and higher paying position, by far. Blacks were denied the right to take the educational courses needed to pass the technical test to become a building engineer.

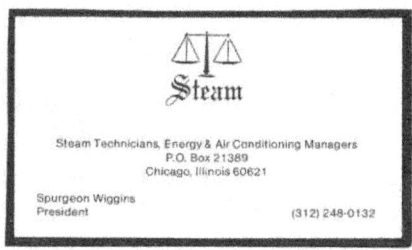

Spurgeon's business card

Dressed for a steam dinner dance

So, an astute group of Black males that worked as firemen and custodians for the Board of Education, formed a study group to compensate for the courses they were denied. My astute husband was one of those founders.

The group, who called themselves S.T.E.A.M. (Steam Technicians, Energy & Air Conditioning Managers), gained force quickly in membership and power. Before the year was up, Black males, as well as other minorities, passed the tests to become engineers for the Chicago Board of Education. Spurgeon earned his stripes, again, becoming president of STEAM, which proudly educated many an individual to help him obtain a fair shake in life.

The grand success of Spurgeon's life did not depend on a set of circumstances. His life shows that we are *far* more than our "lot" in life. We can rise above our challenges with persistence and fortitude. And as Christians we have the added benefit that we know there is a plan for us that will not harm us but profit us with hope and a future (Jeremiah 29:11, paraphrased). Having that assurance helps, when life is unfortunate and scary.

What I found immensely attractive about this fine, brown-framed man was his wholesome thinking, his outlandish smile, and Boy Scout looks. He was a clean-cut American man, the boy next door all grown up. And he loved me!

I hadn't felt special to anyone like this since my incredible Uncle Al was around. Every time I think of him, time freezes to memories of the many furloughs from his army career that he spent at our home. He had such a pure love. We all adored him in our household. He was in his mid-twenties when my brothers and I were orphaned. He wanted to adopt me when I was up for grabs, but he wasn't married at the time and strict 1950s laws forbad it. Nonetheless, my uncle's love for me was unmitigated, and he made me feel valued. I think he had the knack of making people feel like the center of his world.

Our incomparable Uncle Al with all his adoring nieces and nephews.
I am the lucky one in his arms, sitting on the floor.

And, I was indeed special to Spurgeon, whose love for me was also unmitigated. And he, ever thorough, set the stage for a proposal prior to my returning to the city. He told me he wanted me to think about three poignant questions before arriving: 1. Could I deal (happily) long-term with a partner seventeen years older, who had three girls with whom he had strong relationships? 2. What was my philosophy concerning household finances? 3. Could I really handle the challenges of a culturally mixed marriage?

The day I returned to Chicago, I answered his questions to his satisfaction. I brought articles I had collected in Minnesota on the general character of a summer/winter marriage and other articles about stepparent/stepchildren relationships.

We learned that in a marriage with a wide age gap, the younger of the two tends to mature faster and the older tends to enjoy a more energetic life, staying young to a later age.

Concerning stepmoms and stepchildren, the general consensus of all the articles was that it is difficult, relationally, at best, and requires prayer, love, and grace in consideration of each other's needs. Fortunate is the person who manages to develop a good relationship with any or all of the stepchildren. Thankfully, long-term happiness of the biological parent is frequently an influencing factor. I told Spurgie that I would like to fill in the empty spaces in his life, not take over someone else's spot in his heart.

Spurgeon and his three girls: Spurgina, Linda, and Crystal

The financial discussion was the shortest. I proposed we throw both our hard-earned checks in the same pot and plan a workable budget out of the whole that we both could agree with. Then, tithe, bank, and stick to our decisions. That was what he was looking for. End of subject. He wanted to avoid the "What's yours is mine, and what is mine is mine" mentality.

Concerning the matter of becoming a "mixed couple," that was so inconsequential to us, and so consequential to others, that I will devote the next chapter to that discussion.

Back at the drawing board, Spurgeon answered my questions and concerns. I told him that I hated shaving my legs. He said that leg shaving was optional in the Black culture, and he would be great with a blade never again touching my beautiful legs!

That won my heart! I told him I loved him only for his body and good looks. He barely batted an eye, quickly responding with his signature smile and, "That's a great place to start!"

I was impressed that he was certain to not make the same mistake twice. That, of course, is the reason many second marriages fail. But his next subject matter caught me off guard and threw me for a loop! Man, this guy had been doing a lot of thinking! "We should discuss sex," he announced with a twinkle and a grin.

"Like, what about sex needs discussion?" I was game and curious.

"Like, how much love-making do you think is normal?" he wondered aloud.

"Spurgeon," I blurted out, "that's pretty darn regimented to say how often we will make love! Whatever happened to spontaneity?"

He gazed at me, smiling genuinely, and continued: "Well, I would like to know, more or less, say, how many times a week do you think is normal? I don't want to expect too much of you. And I certainly don't want too little from you. So, what do you think is normal?"

Finding this conversation amazingly amusing, I answered, "Well that's difficult to say. Are you talking about the honeymoon, the first couple of years, or ten years from now? Three decades from now? I assume sex drives must fluctuate over the years."

"I mean overall, like an average," still sporting that boy-like grin, the one that lit up his face.

He was determined to pursue this subject to a satisfied end. What an amusing approach toward intimacy. It provided a whole platform for discussion that went on for hours. It was a fun talk; one I've never had before! One I won't forget!

That was Spurgeon in a nutshell. He was the consummate gentleman. The way he handled that talk reminded me of the same manners God uses when He is knocking on the hearts door in Revelation 3:20. He uses a tense of the word *stand* and *knock* (in Greek) that means He is constantly standing and constantly knocking at our heart's door, ardently, as an ongoing act. God is a gentleman, and even though He could burst through any door, He is polite and stands knocking until we respond to the invitation.

God and His child, Spurgie, both gentlemen.

He made me laugh every time he pulled his favorite bedtime one-liner. When he yawned, sighed, or moaned I might ask, out of genuine concern: "Tired, Honey?"

"Not *too* tired!" came his immediate response, always with that grin.

Oh, my, such a healthy hubby! The simple thought process of him immediately thinking of sex amused and delighted me. In Spurgeon's eyes and heart, I was the object of his desires and affections.

In his desire for me, I found my own beauty.

That amazed me.

I had carried the burden of self-deprecation for so many years. In His trusting love for me, I was free to manifest the full spectrum of that which God made me to be, and thereby fulfill myself as well as Spurgeon. Real men encourage their wives to be real women, with their words or deeds and love. So, it ends up being a constant cycle of love and growth in a healthy marriage.

After that conversation culminated, I figured that all the seriousness was over, and we could proceed with the lighter stuff. But he had one more hefty pronouncement. With gravity, he held my hands, peering deeply into my eyes. "I am crazy about you. I will love you and treat you well forever. Just don't make a fool of me."

Ouch! Wow! Man! Harsh!

I learned something that exact moment. That stunning example of a man had been deeply bruised. He wanted to make sure history did not repeat itself.

Mm, mm, mm. Smart guy. Delicious and smart and godly and funny and tender . . . and vulnerable.

And I didn't have to shave my legs ever again! Yes!

Spurgeon and I immediately made a pact of fidelity and devotion to each other with a little ceremony before God. We called it our *covenant*. We wondered about the wedding in Canaan where Jesus turned water to wine. We wondered if, at that time, weddings were only a religious matter or a legal procedure, or both. It had been two years since I had left my marriage, but it would be a long time before my divorce would come through. With hearts free and clear, we moved in together and married as soon as we could.

The Mutual Admiration Society of Spurgeon and Deb was officially founded on July 26, 1984.

CHAPTER 4

Settling In

WE WERE OVER THE moon about our togetherness and picking out our wedding rings. We wanted nothing to do with over-the-counter wedding bands and went completely rogue. Neither of us wore jewelry, so we decided these rings would be the one and only center of attention in the adornment department. We went to the designers, Jan Dee Jewelers, in Chicago.

At Jan Dee's, they helped us get a look that we appreciated. Ruby is the stone of our choice. We wanted a solitary ruby, beveled, with a loose, rope like design that intertwines. We wanted a ruby because it reminded us of our great sin and our great passion for God and one another.

The desired color in a ruby is "pigeon blood red," a deep hue that increases with the depth of the stone. It takes a larger ruby to be pretty than it does a diamond. The facets of a diamond show off the light and shine on the surface, but the ruby must have weight and depth to achieve the idyllic red. We liked weight and depth in what we were and did. We took our time and waited for the stones that had our names on them.

A couple of times a month, the store received a shipment of new stones and called us in to see if one or two of them drew our attention. After many visits, our idyllic rings arrived. We enjoyed wearing one piece of art on our bodies, and these pieces received a great deal of attention over the years. People were intrigued with the selection and solitary design.

Settling in to life with the man with the matching ring was fascinating! He was *absolute* joy. This wonderful man of God spoke lovingly and excelled in communication. He was clean cut, and kindness exuded through his pores. He daily exhibited gentility and sported a stellar attitude. That *joie de vivre* he carried everywhere made him especially attractive.

He was interested in everything that came out of my mouth, and we spent hours sharing, laughing, recollecting, and telling our life stories to each other. In his arms I was safe and loved.

We found it fascinating to see how single-minded we were. Harmony dominated each new aspect of our lives. I related to everything that came out of his mouth, and he totally got me! He got my heart! He sensed my intents were positive. I pinched myself often, just to see if this was really happening.

One of our earliest team efforts was adoption of a World Vision child. We decided we'd take any child they gave us. (Sometimes people pick the little, cute kids, and the older or less physically attractive ones get left behind.) When one child grew out of the system, we picked up another. We picked World Vision because of their financial integrity. Eighty two percent of the dollar goes directly to the child, and only eighteen percent is spent on administration. It doesn't get any better than that.

We also looked ahead in regard to digging a well in a needy area of the world. We agreed that one day, we would, by God's grace, dig a well thru World Vision. But we were content with supporting a family at the time. (See CHAPTER 17: "Fun Stuff," for more on the well-building plan.)

Fortunately, he wanted healthy meals and pitched in on the cooking regularly. We both worked, we both rehabbed the house, and we both cleaned and cooked.

We thought of ourselves as gourmands and liked to treat each other, and others, with dishes that the other had never encountered.

He was hands down the egg maker of the family, but by far, his greatest contributions to our good health were his fabulous meals of greens and smoked turkey necks.

Okra, a vegetable formerly unknown to me, became a versatile staple. Stewed, fried, or as flavor enhancer or thickener in a dish, okra became a favorite. The taste is exquisite. The slime . . . well, that is a matter of overcoming!

Persimmon, with its cotton candy sweetness and looking something like the tomato family, became a favorite fruit. Spurgie said the kids in the hood picked them wild and snacked on them, as they grew on bushes near the woods in Mississippi. He had a knack for picking out the best selections in the market up North.

Fried, green tomatoes became a seasonal front-runner. We have a girlfriend, Carol, who made a point of coming over several times a year with her green tomatoes so we could all eat Spurgie's famous fried, green tomatoes.

He dipped the tomatoes in eggs and milk before dunking them in the cornmeal batter. But the culminating touch is something we three encountered by accident: We grabbed a ripe avocado, sliced that on top of the Southern treat and discovered a meal worth raving about. We repeated this more times than we care to admit!

We ate straight out of Spurgie's magnificent garden of opulence as much as we could. Ruth (our unofficial granddaughter and heart-girl) is the daughter of a family who adopted us when we moved to Southwest Michigan. She loved to come in the spring when our peapods begged to be picked. We ate them raw, in salads, or in Chinese-style food, sautéed with garlic and soy sauce.

When the corn was ripe, we ate whole meals of corn-on-the-cob for a couple of days, accompanied only by salt and butter or parmesan cheese. His organic corn was so sweet that, while we held the cooked cobs and nibbled, our fingers stuck together with its syrup. Everyone who lived with us liked this odd gourmet habit.

When his little pickling cucumbers were ripe, we ate vinegar and cuke salads until they came out of our ears! Having eaten our way through Spurgie's opulent gardens of wellness, I felt so healthy when our wholesome summers drew to an end.

When the beefsteak and Roma tomatoes peaked, we had BLTs for dinner three days in a row. We all liked this healthy gorging.

The food traditions that I brought to the table from Norwegian culture were far less nutritious but no less delicious. *Coumpa*, for example, is a delectable potato dumpling, cooked up with ham. It is high carb, high fat, a bit bland, and is a tasty comfort food in the Scando community.

Lefse, a potato tortilla of a sort, is dry-fried on a very hot griddle and rolled up with butter and sugar. It is hands down the favorite Scando food of most Minnesotans. With *coumpa* and *lefse* being both potato dishes, Spurgie was introduced to more white potatoes than he had ever eaten. While growing up, his main starch was rice.

From *lefse* we skip to the line of bakery treats that are perhaps better known: *Sandbakkels* are a crisp cookie prepared in a corrugated metal tin, *krumkake* and rosettes are both made with hot irons. Spurgeon was not much of a sweet eater, but he enjoyed these cultural icons of Minnesota each Christmas because they were an extension of me. We made plates of these Christmas goodies to give to the neighbors, just like my Mom Hildur did when she was alive.

We laughed about one memorable cross-culture habit that both of our families shared regarding coffee drinking. The seniors in Spurgie's Mississippi life drank coffee from a cup and saucer. But instead of sipping the coffee from the cup, they poured the contents onto the saucer, put their heads down and slurped! And that is exactly the way the old Scandos in Minnesota drank their coffee! Most kids think this is a great habit, and they readily join in the action!

Though we shared the slurping custom in both cultures, Spurgeon found a habit of my biological family amusing. The minute a car pulled up in their driveway, the hosts pulled out a coffee mug for each passenger and poured cups of java for the visitors before their feet hit the threshold! Spurgie said it reminded him of his uncle who exhibited the identical habit with his moonshine!

With both of us interested in gourmet cooking, we decided to have a food tradition where we could put our skills together. We planned an annual gathering where friends and family could join in a celebration of God's goodness. It was a reflective time of thanksgiving, with stories about how the couples met and got together. We mutually chose seafood gumbo as the main dish because it is so exotic, though he had a great deal more acquaintance with this dish than I. Each year around Valentine's Day, we would ask couples from the community, the church, the neighborhood, and family, in order to have a potpourri of guests. The idea was to not invite the same couple twice.

First, we sent out invitations a month ahead of the date. When the time arrived, we spent three days preparing the gumbo, pulling out the biggest pot we had in the house. The first day we went to the seafood market and grocery store to buy the twenty-seven ingredients in the gumbo recipe. The second day we prepped all the food, slicing and dicing, while we cleaned the house from top to bottom. The third day we started the roux at 11:00 in the morning. The giant pot simmered all day until the 6:00 o'clock dinner guests arrived.

In those gumbo years, a tremendous variety of people crossed our threshold! Everyone from near and far, family, our mechanic, the chief of police, neighbors, a college administrator, church family, a local judge, the sheriff, the refuse guy, the mailman and many more. They all sat together in the dining room, ate gumbo off depression-era glass plates, and shared as if they were old friends.

Our gumbo recipe came from an old cookbook a friendly couple gave me when we lived in New Orleans for three months. (Should you want to try your hand at this culinary delight, I have included the recipe in the last chapter of the book, "Fun Stuff.")

This was always a highlight of our year, as guests enjoyed it tremendously. It helped brighten the dark days of our Michigan winter, while giving honor to love and marriage. We carried on this tradition for twenty-four years, until the workload became too much.

I knew Spurgeon acted well, worked hard, and was kind, compassionate, and generous. So, this is what a *real* man acts like? This wonder-boy glow, deep understanding, and patience with my immaturity was just who he was. One day I asked him, "How did you get to be so loving and kind, when you came from the background you did?"

His response was immediate: "Oh, it wasn't what I did. It was what God did. I was a young believer, and He brought me through it all."

Clearly, he knew who he was and Whose he was. I started to see him as my role model.

"Did you have any role models growing up?" I asked.

"Well, the closest I came to a role model was a young man who was just a couple years older than me and lived nearby," he replied.

"You are pretty together yourself. What was it about him that made you admire him so?" I asked.

"Oh, wow, he could do everything with such ease, excelling at anything he put his hand to, always with a big smile on his face. I would try and race with him, and he beat me every time, grinning all the while. Didn't matter if he was picking cotton, he'd pick it faster than me. Planting a field, he'd finish his row in double time. If he was singing at church, his tonal quality surpassed everyone's. Whatever he put his hand to, it turned to gold."

"Whatever became of him, do you know?" I wondered.

Sadness entered the room. Then, in a hushed, respectful tone: "Well, when he was about nineteen, he was found down by the river, reportedly drowned, under strange circumstances."

"What do you mean, strange circumstances?" I inquired gently, as his eyes darkened with pain.

"He swam with stamina and skill. And yet his body was badly bruised and beaten, tossed like a piece of refuse on the riverbank, left for dead." Even after all these years, Spurgeon was crestfallen as he shared this.

It has been speculated that White males do not hate Black males, so much as they fear them because of their skills and formidability.

With all the cultural obstacles that American history has imposed upon Blacks, they have refused to lie down and die. Instead, Black Americans have steadily risen to excellence in many fields, despite obvious oppression.

I wondered if this ugly fear was at play so many years ago at the river in Mississippi.

Praise God, Spurgeon Wiggins Jr., had a chance to grow up! I am eternally grateful for a husband who lived his life making good choices and "fleeing from evil." I praise God for His hand of protection over this marvelous man so that he could live a full life, leaving us his tenderness, love, and wisdom.

Oh, his playfulness and humor should not be overlooked! Proof of this came each time we entered an elevator alone together. Something about this mischievously romantic man-made elevator rides hilarious!

In the city, we frequently found ourselves in tall buildings with long elevator rides. The first time, we were dressed to the nines and rising in the shaft. Spurgeon waited for the doors to close, then deftly lit upon me, firmly grasped my waist with his left arm, pinned me against the wall, and slid his right arm under my thigh. He moved down to my knee, pulling my leg up around his thigh as he passionately devoured my neck and lips! All of this in one swift, smooth, athletic motion!

Initially, I was taken aback, but enjoyed being swept off my feet for the first time in my life! I then became paranoid the door would open, so I pushed him away. He backed up politely and eyeballed my dress to be sure it was covering all the leg he had exposed. He stared into my eyes, winked, and stood as erect as a soldier. He smiled like an angel, as the elevator door slid open.

I have no idea what inspired Spurgeon to repeat that behavior on similar occasions. If we were only rising a couple floors, he would eyeball me as the door closed and ask, "Do you dare me?"

"Absolutely not!" was my adamant response. But I adored his romantic advances on the long runs. He was never sleazy or inappropriate, just tender and amorous. And the funny thing is, he had the timing down so well that we never got caught! (I am supposing that all those years ago there were no security cameras watching this hot affection.)

Not surprisingly, Spurgeon was always on my team, first up to bat. He saw the best in me and encouraged me in all my pursuits. We became a force to reckon with. He called us the "A Team." When our grandkids stayed with us for stretches of time, and we adopted our son, we all became the "A Team."

Spurgeon Wiggins Jr. was so sure of himself; he didn't blink an eye when he found I am a bit . . . unusual. I attribute my oddities to being "a peculiar people," as God expresses it. Secondly, the Designer made me an artist, and we, admittedly, often march to the beat of a different drummer. "Size large character," "eccentric," "quirky," "weird." Most artists answer to all those adjectives and more. I'm good with that, but it does take a strong character to value those traits in others. Spurgeon saw in me what most people label odd, and he understood and found my oddities refreshing. He often told me that I was fearless. He was right.

I don't have enough imagination to be somebody that I'm not. Easier to just be me. And that can, at times, be a bold statement.

The boots we both like

One day I needed warm winter boots. I found an ostentatious pair in a fake, white polar bear style. Excited that the store had them in my size 10 1/2 foot, I tried them on and paraded for Spurgie in the store, asking what he thought.

He put on his iridescent smile, accompanied with eye-sparkles, and appreciatively stated, "I married such a unique woman!"

He was a genius in navigating life's journey. And he brought me with him.

We served as best we knew, delighted in the Lord and delighted in our lives together. Our three-strand cord was a good, working unit: God, Spurgeon, and I.

CHAPTER 5

The Interracial Climate of the Early 1980s

I observed that Black Americans, when in monochromatic groups, spend little to no time speaking of the daily occurrences of prejudice and slights. They happen with such frequency that to comment on the same would keep one's mind in a dark place. People don't want to stay there. Smart. Very smart. Pick your battles.

Mixed racial couples receive roughly the same amount of negative attention as monochromatic Black couples. But the reality is that we faced it, just like Americans of color have done all these years, wherever possible. We ignored the stupidity.

Truth be told, Spurgeon and I were so thrilled to be together, we couldn't imagine anyone inhibiting our love for each other. We were rubber, and everything bounced off us without the least bit of anger or wasted energy. However, Spurgeon's lifelong experiences in the world of racism gave me a heads-up on how to handle the negativity without anger.

Back in the early '80s, Chicago sported very few interracial couples. Shockingly, we did not know even one other mixed pair. And did we get the stares! Mr. Cool, Calm, and Collected coached me in this matter: "They have a problem, Sweetheart. Let it remain their problem."

Brilliant! It became part of my philosophy. I love it when ideas work!

One time, we went to Spurgie's brother's wedding in the city. It was a cultural experience for me, and I looked forward to the jumping over the broom. This is a long-standing tradition among Black Americans. Since they could not legally marry for 250 years under slavery, they created a tradition of newlyweds jumping over a broom to signifying a leap into a new life.

In a post-wedding conversation, I heard someone ask the bride, "Mabel, you have owned your home in that rough, West side neighborhood for decades. Don't you ever get scared?"

Shaking her head from side to side she replied: "Nah. I walk with a gun in one hand and a Bible in the other, and I use whichever one I need to first!" Though I did not have the privilege of getting to know Mabel, I believe she spoke the truth. You have to be ready for anything and use creativity, especially in order to stay positive in negative situations.

The following is a story of a memorable day regarding overt prejudice. I chose this tale because it ends in a positive note, unlike most incidences of such nature.

Initially, we rented a garden apartment in a changing, old Polish neighborhood. Our landlord, named Art, delighted in establishing the United Nations in his end of the block.

We plopped a swing for two in the pretty little courtyard

Art owned two three-flat buildings next door to each other with an empty garden space in between. This space had housed a building which had burned down in prior decades. In our building alone lived Blacks, Whites, Chinese and Mexicans. It was a wonderful palette of mixed skin tones.

We plopped a swing for two in the pretty little courtyard, planted some flowers, and ate from the raspberry patch in the rear of the lot. For an apartment, it was fabulously relaxing. We even had a wood-burning fireplace that actually functioned.

This was the 1980s, and The Windy City was said to be the most segregated city in the nation. Interracial neighborhoods were an innovation in Chicago during that era, and we liked the changes we saw in this segment of the city. After two years, we found an abandoned building in Bucktown, a near-North neighborhood. It was located a mile from our apartment, with great bones, and we bought it. Close to one of our jobs, the price was right. Repairs were needed and we were the team to take that on.

The first floor was a breeze, as we only needed to raise the ceilings to their original heights by removing the old, lowered ceiling panels along with their metal rigging. We then filled the screw holes, painted the house with a spray paint gun, and hung a ceiling fan with lights. We started on our upstairs residence, after we put another family downstairs.

The upstairs needed the ceilings lifted also, but this was an easy job in our youth. The more laborious jobs were laying hexagonal ceramic tiles in the kitchen and sanding and varnishing all the oak floors throughout the house. Fortunately, all the original woodwork was present, even if we did have to retrieve the pocket doors from the basement. The built-in China cabinet and the working fireplace were constructed of beautiful oak and ash. They lent well to a good cleaning and some Danish oil.

After a couple weeks of hitting hard this rehabbing, we decided we needed a break on a lovely, spring day. So, we ventured on a long walk to get to know our neighborhood. Inside that four-mile jaunt, we encountered three instances of interracial reaction. Two were highly distasteful, but we let them keep their problems. The last one was unexpected and amusing.

Spurgeon decided to stop at a corner dive to purchase his occasional lotto ticket. I fancied enjoying a few stores on antique row.

We stepped into the dirty, little, corner café, and the greasy-haired cook/waiter/manager/owner at the cash register mocked loudly, "Well, what do we have here?" in a Smoky Mountains accent so thick you could slice it.

As Dolly Parton accurately states, "It's hard to be a diamond in a rhinestone world."

Spurgeon politely responded, "You have someone who wants a lotto ticket, sir."

Staring at my husband wryly, then swallowing me up in his lurid eyes, the filthy man in the grimy white apron guffawed and completed the transaction.

We left, feeling sorry for the poor soul who could scarcely look in the mirror and say he loved himself.

On to the antique shops.

We had fun looking and found an old, rusty lamp at a garage sale. Having made arrangements to bring that home, we sallied on to the rest of our walking trip.

After about a half-mile, we spotted three young, White males approaching on the sidewalk from the opposite direction. They were verbose and seemed menacing, even from afar. And, sure enough, coming closer, they stepped three broad, hooked arms in solidarity, and continued their charge, chuckling to one another.

Insecure people do stupid things. Then they turn around and think they are smart!

Our names are not written on any portion of the city sidewalks, so we were more than happy to move so they wouldn't mow us over. We stepped to the side and let the three smirking young men pass. They were very pleased with themselves.

We were pleased with ourselves too. After the sidestep, we returned to the sidewalk, hooked raised arms in an exaggerated manner, and goose-stepped, laughing at ourselves. Spurgie winked at me, and I reacted with a beaming smile.

Let it remain their problem. Smart.

We try to avoid the term "race" when speaking of varied cultural groups. We contend that there is only one race, the human race, and we are all part of that. Drinking people of all cultures tend to create more drama than we are willing to deal with, so we stay away from any group of alcohol-imbibing people, no matter their "cultural identity," the term we use instead of "race."

Only about a mile before home, we spotted a tavern up ahead on our side of the street. We have a standing family rule not to go near such places. We thought of crossing the street to avoid the man who gingerly came out of the bar, but were anxious to get home, so we stayed the course.

The approaching White guy had the bounciest gait I'd ever seen on a man. He must have been about in his early thirties and walked with a pronounced swag. He stared at us intently, scrutinizing us from afar. His gaze intensified as we neared him.

As we braced ourselves for yet another insult, the stranger, now ten feet away, suddenly stopped, jumped in his own tracks, planted his feet firmly, put on a radiant glow with arms raised, and loudly declared: "Wow! What a *great* looking couple!"

He kept on beaming, hands raised, as he passed us. We merrily returned his smile.

"Life is like a box of mixed chocolates," we mutually agreed. You never know when one of those average-looking morsels is going to leave the best taste in your mouth.

That same month, on a spring weekend evening, we attended an annual dinner/dance in a banquet hall. We ended up sitting at a table of all White women, some older than Spurgeon. This was not anything unusual for him. I had seen him many times sit in the midst of a circle of aunties, sisters, daughters, or nieces, and he had been the male equivalent of the belle of the ball. Here, he affably engaged this table of ladies with his gorgeous smile and easy conversation.

As Spurgeon rose from his seat, he faced me and gently bowed while extending his hand: "May I have the pleasure, my dear?"

As I rose to dance with him in his suave Italian suit and my pretty-in-polka-dots dress, the ladies at the table smiled approvingly and whispered amongst themselves. The Staple Singers sang "Respect Yourself" as we danced "The Bump," the rage at the time.

Returning to the table, Spurgeon told the circle of ladies he was going to get a couple drinks for us and would anyone like something? With no takers, he jaunted off.

Dancing the night away

The matriarch of the table, seated next to me, immediately leaned my way and quietly began a short soliloquy.

"Honey, I'm not in favor of interracial dating or marriages. But if a man that good looking and charming paid that much attention to me, I wouldn't care if he were purple with orange polka dots! Good for you!"

And herein lies the key to a happy woman: Husbands, pay attention to your wives and be perpetually polite. Your wives will be tickled at the attention you pay them, and you will teach an important skill to those poor husbands who don't have an inkling of how to make their wives happy.

Occasionally, we treated each other to explorative trips to New York City for cultural highlights. The Big Apple appealed to our theatrical tastes and our cuisine curiosity, as well as our sense of adventure. We attended Broadway plays, and tripped to Grand Central

Station, Liberty Island, Rockefeller Center, the Metropolitan Museum of Art, and many other sites embodied in Manhattan Island.

To scale replica of Lady Liberty's face

Central Park is an absorbing place during the day and provides the Big Apple with a nature conservatory in the middle of the most populated city in North America. We learned that it is one of the places where Americans actually stroll.

The definition of stroll is "to walk in a leisurely way, to amble." The art and beauty of the stroll is extinct in North American culture. We tend to walk for health or necessity. But in Central Park, everybody believes the 843 acres of lush green is for pure enjoyment. Though it is only the fifth-largest preserve in New York City, it is the most frequently visited park in the entire world with an excess of 42,000,000 people taking it in annually.

In the park strolling, we saw bird watchers, heard music in the outdoor amphitheater, and watched roller bladers jump trash barrels for competition. We enjoyed joggers of all styles, mimes, and mini street shows where the money hat was present.

A particularly sunny day found us mesmerized by barrel jumpers. We sat down to watch skilled teens of every creed and color compete with one another. No more had we found a bird's-eye-view-bench to sit upon, when a young man with a cast on his leg sat next to us, immediately engaging us in conversation.

"Man, any other day it would be me you'd be watching," the friendly teen smiled in our direction.

"Is that [pointing to his cast] how you got hurt?" we wondered aloud.

"Yup! And it's killin' me to not be out there! I live for this stuff!" The cute teen shared unreservedly. He said he was from Puerto Rico and was going to have to knuckle down and get serious about a job now that he was graduating from high school. He had his parents' approval to hang out in the park this last free summer. He had only three more days on the crutches and cast; then he would be liberated. We agreed he was the true definition of "chomping at the bit."

Interestingly, we did not find one ugly racial incident in our four visits to this East Coast Apple. Quite the contrary. People stopped us on the streets wanting to help us or share their personal opinions. Many New York City residents defy the stereotype of being cold and rude. We found them to be interested in us and helpful at the drop of a hat.

I suppose that the difference is because New York is the quintessential melting pot, and the mixed ethnic varieties make a fragrant potpourri. The scent of this bouquet of cultures is alluring and mesmerizing, so people get along.

That's my theory and I'm sticking to it!

Early one New York morning, we set out to Liberty Island. No more had we whipped out our transportation map of the city than a young man came up to us and asked us where we wanted to go. He gave us perfect directions, suggested a quick breakfast place before the ferry, ordered us to have fun, and off we went.

A couple of days later we headed to China town. As we stood on the corner waiting for a bus, deeply absorbed in our book, <u>New York on $100 a Day</u>, a darling little Jewish lady with *babushka* and thick Yiddish accent asked us, "Where do you want to go?"

Answering that we would like authentic Chinese food, she named her favorite. Then, while waiting for the bus, she told us how to and how *not* to pick a restaurant in New York City. She advised us to watch where a desired ethnic group goes to eat. [If we want Chinese, see which restaurants have a high density of *those* people dining there.] She said to not be fooled by fancy tablecloths and high-priced places because heavy competition insures low prices for good food. And use the bathroom before ordering. The kitchen will have the same cleanliness as the bathrooms.

We never forgot that advice, nor her. She was so warm and concerned with our needs, she could almost have adopted us.

She sent us off with a smile, wave, and her last declaration, arm raised with pointing finger extended: "Now remember, kids, you don't eat the tablecloths!"

We have often shared that advice with others and laughed at the memory of our warm-hearted, ten-minute, New York City friend.

Little Italy in Manhattan is our place for a hearty Italian meal. On the bus one day, with our <u>New York on $100 a Day</u> in hand, someone asked us what we sought. Replying we were looking for a good place to eat in Little Italy, the gentleman next to us insisted we go to his favorite restaurant. He added that President Reagan had just been there, and they had named a couple of dishes after him.

Then a guy across the bus aisle a couple seats down argued, "No, no, don't go there, go to *Antonio's*. You can't go wrong."

Then came a *third* person with yet another opinion that joined the debate!

Three New Yorkers sat in the sparsely populated bus and, with good natured smiles, bantered about where the two of us should spend our evening meal! It was riotous!

Back in our room, Spurgeon and I observed, again, that New Yorkers seemed much more open than Chicagoans when it came to mixed couples. We said it was because the Big Apple is comprised of the whole world. Everyone there is used to the mix.

Back in Chicago's Bucktown at 1942 Oakdale, we enjoyed a retired neighbor, Wayne, who gleefully introduced himself as an "old hillbilly." He loved to hang out in the alley and talk with anyone who passed. His hang spot was behind his garage, right across the alley from our fenced-in yard, so he and Spurgeon often chatted about our building rehab or whatever old men talk about.

That adorable "hillbilly" called out to Spurgie any time he saw him coming, always in his thick hills accent, "Well here comes my beeesst buddy!" They fell into a fast and trusting relationship.

On one occasion, as Spurgeon and I walked by, the always-upbeat Wayne had a beef to air. He said he was irritated with Hank, an old guy in the hood who walked his dog down our alley daily. Spurgie asked why he was peeved.

"Ah, he thinks he can tell me how to run my business. He told me I shouldn't talk with you because you are Black!"

"What did you say to that?" Spurgeon gently inquired.

"Why, I told him in no uncertain terms that I will talk to any man, woman, or dog that I want to!" These words were adamantly spoken.

And so, the friendship between hillbilly Wayne and Spurgeon thrived.

There were many elements of people living in newly renovated Bucktown. Not all were good to know.

A solid year after we moved to the neighborhood, our home was broken into. Spurgeon told Wayne about the break-in, to alert him in case the thieves were working the neighborhood.

Wayne lowered his head and listened earnestly. With regret in his voice, he stated, "Yeah, well, I could tell you something that might ease your mind in that regard."

"Oh, yeah? Like what?" Spurgeon asked.

"Do you remember Hank, with his dog?"

"Yeah, sure. What about him?"

Wayne lifted his head, looked Spurgeon in the eyes and said, "The two neighborhood thugs that broke into your place told Hank to tell you not to worry. They are like lightning and only strike once in the same place."

As far as we knew, they were true to their word. Big cities can sometimes be like small towns. Everybody knows everything in the barrio. In the country, what you perceive to be a wolf may sometimes be a dog. In the city, it is the opposite; the "dogs" are, at times, "wolves."

It was interesting to learn from each other's cultures, and, happy to put on rose-tinted glasses, we did just that.

One giant difference I saw between Blacks and Whites was the menu at a picnic. In Minnesota, a large gathering would include a dozen salads and side dishes with the mandatory gelatin salad and deviled eggs, half a dozen desserts, a couple of homemade breads, and a meat or two.

In picnics given by Black Americans you will have six different kinds of meat, most of them grilled. The meats are accompanied by macaroni and cheese and a big, beautiful pot of greens. A single dessert is often presented, usually a lemon pound cake or banana pudding made with vanilla wafers. Both spreads were inviting to us!

Where the two ethnic groups spend vacations, there is a huge gulf. Spurgeon said most Blacks fly to a major city to enjoy the trappings, while Whites tend to drive to remote places like lakes and cottages and state or national parks.

But Spurgeon was different from most Blacks, as he plunged into remote areas like frogs jump into water. We went where we wanted to and minded our own business. And we shared campfires with friendlies. We were happy to enjoy nature and each other.

Five years after our original covenant we moved to Michigan. Quite naïve, we encountered an unanticipated, mixed bag of tricks.

Our immediate neighbor welcomed us the day after we moved with a homemade welcome cake and card, but other neighbors were quietly menacing. We started getting crank calls at three in the morning. The bedroom telephone was on Spurgie's side of the bed. Thinking it could be an emergency, Spurgeon picked up the phone, to hear a caller snarling, "Hey, n- - - - -, who says anyone wants you in the neighborhood?"

After a half-dozen of those middle-of-the-night wake-up incidents, they ceased. We're pretty sure we know who it was. They never laid hands on us, though.

This next story could have taken place anywhere in the U.S., but it happened at a nearby state park.

We had evolved over the years from camping with a pup tent to a pop-up trailer, then a camper. We bought a beautiful turquoise pickup to pull our twenty-four foot Canadian-made camper. We were then ready to take the sharp little duo out for a maiden voyage.

On our drive through the campground to find a spot to suit our needs, we noted that all the adult, male campers had long, stringy, dirty hair. Their fully tattooed appendages reflected the beers and drugs they toted, as they passed around a funny-type of cigarette. We felt the weight of animosity as we toured the grounds. Parking tentatively outside the circle of campers, we walked down to the river to talk. Momentarily, an amiable young man who had neither greasy, long hair nor tattoos walked to the river spot and engaged us in an open conversation.

I can't remember how the exchange switched subjects so drastically, but the next words out of this kind man's mouth were: "You know, guys, far be it for me to tell you what to do. But I watched you as you drove through the campground looking for a spot, and it was painful for me to see the hostility that met you. I hate to say this, but I fear for your safety if you stay. It looks like the best thing you could do at this moment is to get back in your truck and go find another place to enjoy your weekend. I smell trouble for you if you don't. And I am so sorry to have this conversation with you."

We felt his concern, took him up on his suggestion, and left for higher ground. We thanked God, again, for the kindness of a complete stranger.

The fact that most Black Americans vacation in cities, while Whites enjoy anywhere they want, is rooted in our history, of course. Back in the 1920s through the 1950s, Black Americans were not allowed to stay in most hotels nor eat in most restaurants. This unspoken rule extended into the 1960s and even early 1970s. Accommodations for Blacks could be found by using the _Green Book_, a booklet used in that era to guide Blacks to places where they were welcomed.

After the civil rights movement in the '60s, the U.S. government mandated all commercial businesses to allow Blacks to use their facilities. Large chain businesses made the change immediately, and African Americans, belatedly, began to patronize those chains. Mom-and-Pop businesses tended to hold out longer with their varied forms of segregation.

Jews often experienced the same problem in that era. A prime example: A friend of ours, Steve, an antique buff, was cleaning out the basement of an old resort here in Southwestern Michigan when he ran across stacks of vintage advertisements concerning that resort. The first stack was in the '20s and '30s, as it stated, "Refrigerators are supplied with ice blocks on a daily basis." The last sentence on the flyer was, "Absolutely no Jews."

The second flyer must have been printed in the '40s and '50s, as electric lights and range and running water were mentioned. The culminating line in this ad was, "Gentiles preferred."

The third and last flyer found was, perhaps, used in the '60s and beyond. The cabins at this point had a "toilet room with lavatory and flush closets." The last sentence on this ad was, "Carefully selected clientele."

Perhaps Jews used the _Green Book_ also.

CHAPTER 6

Seeking the Plan Together

THOUGH CHICAGO WAS A fabulous place for both of us regarding vocations, cultural variety, plentiful arts, and great ethnic foods, we were both country bumpkins at heart. So as soon as we got back from our camping honeymoon, we sat down in prayer and discussed getting back to our roots and possibly leaving Chicago for a warmer climate. He had job offers with the American Aviation Association in Washington State and New Mexico. My elementary education teaching degree would be versatile anywhere. Though we checked out the Santa Rosa location on our honeymoon, a big problem for us was the entire environment being the color brown in July. We were accustomed to thirty shades of green in the Midwestern states during summer. We switched our attentions to Washington State.

But, rejecting Washington was a quick no-brainer, as well. We would be way too far from our families, who were largely in the Midwest. Since we love plush green, our next thoughts went to Tennessee, as we read that the climate was very comfortable there.

So, we took a week to explore that beautiful emerald of the Smokies. We camped near an equestrian facility and signed up for a whole day on horseback. These newly developed trails revealed a high density of rattlesnakes. A State Park Department of Natural Resources person had to accompany us, because these people were the only ones who could legally kill the protected rattlesnake. We pondered that.

Moreover, the next morning when our tent was covered with hundreds of three-inch centipedes that fell on us as we crawled out, we decided that Michigan was a good place to retire after all. We set our focus back in the Midwest.

We started camping on weekend trips to the Southwestern part of Michigan, only two hours from Chicago. It was stunningly beautiful with fabulous real estate values. We hoped that after five years of concentrated hard work, perhaps we could move to our dream location.

But two divorced people generally start at ground zero financially. So how did we dare think we could pull up stakes and move in such a short period? Ahhh. It was prayer, planning, sticking to the plan, hard work, and more prayer.

We are both financially literate, hardworking, and groomed for success. We developed a formula for saving money to accomplish this move, from which many couples could benefit. It's simple, like us, just in case you'd like to know. Mind you, this worked for two mature, professional, salaried people.

1). Take out all the tax shelter annuities possible from both of your checks and don't touch it. You have 401K? Same idea.

2). Live off of one income. We decided we would live off of his salary because it was bigger than mine, and we could still have fun.

3). Bank or invest the second income, in both names.

4). Buy a fixer-upper with good bones, in both names, in a good neighborhood, and live there while you fix it. Work hard.

5). Tithe. And give offerings.

Now I'm not telling you that there is no sacrifice involved. We also agreed to live frugally. We ate out only once a week, and it had to be under $20 (in the '80s), unless it was a special occasion. We parked the cars and walked or biked everywhere, all weekends. We bought a pup tent and spent a month each summer camping in national parks, getting to know the whole U.S. We did all house repairs ourselves, accumulating sweat equity. We worked full time and rehabbed our abandoned beauty of a house each day until shower and bedtime. We were thrilled to be together and worked hard to have a beautiful life. Dreams were coming true, and we were on top of the world!

I cannot, at this point, undervalue the power of tithing and its economic boost to the household of believers. We attended Faith Tabernacle, a church of 5,000 in the old Marigold Boxing Arena and tithed there. "Taste and see that the Lord is good," says God in Psalms 34:8 (NIV).

We did.

He is.

This does not happen often in life, but all went as we'd planned, perfectly.

We took a break from rehabbing our house one spring day and went to get married.

We dressed to the nines. Spurgeon was debonair in his raw silk suit with silk shirt. He looked edible. I donned a flowing, white silk blouse with a fine cotton embroidered skirt. We felt radiant as we drove to the Chicago downtown civic center. (The cover photo is taken the day of our wedding.)

It was unseasonably hot this ninety-three-degree, mid-May day in Chicago with the humidity nearly the same. We parked in the closest spot possible to the civic center in underground parking on Wacker Drive, but by the time we walked to our destination several blocks away, we were drenched in sweat! This is *not* what you want on your sacred day.

Our silk shirts clung to our wet bodies. On entering the building, we needed to find a spot to cool off and dry out before approaching the justice of the peace.

Afterwards, with the sweat dissipated, we found our way to the matrimonial sanctuary.

Initially, it was evident that we amused the justice of the peace with our presence. But he fast warmed up to us and ultimately accomplished his job with pleasantry.

Arriving at home after the nuptials, we fell into a zesty exchange.

"Well, do you feel more married now?" I queried my handsome groom.

"No, not really. I felt married before the civic center," replied the new husband.

"I felt married the day I returned to Chicago and fell in your arms," I admitted.

"Yup, that did it for me," he agreed.

"Yup. I love you," I agreed, in essence.

Not to be outdone, he assured me, "But, you know that I love you more." And with this he would make me blush as he pursed his lips and threw me a kiss with a wink and a grin. It tickled me every time he did it. I ate it up.

And he did it our whole marriage!

Many times, over the years when new friends asked about our wedding day, they frequently reacted with a sigh and inquiries something like this: "Oh, how sad. Do you ever wish, now, that you had done it differently?"

Both of us agreed, "Never!"

"Really? Why?" insisted the inquiries.

Our response went something like this: "It's a second marriage for both of us, and we were so happy to be together that anyone else's presence would have been superfluous. Besides, the marriage is far more important than the wedding. We had our eyes on something bigger than just that day."

It's funny about people's ideas of nuptials. Some people still went away from the above conversation disappointed that our covenant was not performed in front of a crowd.

Others jumped into the age gap issue. One of my besties queried me with, "Yeah, Deb, are you sure you aren't looking for a father figure? Seventeen years' difference is a lot!"

"I'm not going to deny or reject that possibility," I admitted. "What I am looking for this time around, however, is a man who loves the Lord and thinks that I am absolutely enchanting. And on days that I may not be enchanting, I still want him to believe in me and protect me and work with me, not against me. I think I am good mate potential, and a mature man suits me fine. Besides, I read that it is better to be an old man's princess than a young man's harlot."

The conversation came to an abrupt halt.

But Spurgeon's and my ideas of romance varied drastically from many traditional couples'. We paid huge attention to each other's needs and thrilled at meaningful touches and kisses on a daily basis, but we were both a bit cavalier about missing dated celebrations.

Spurgie normally considered the day I returned to Chicago to be our anniversary date. I more frequently remembered the civic center date. Either way, when one or the other forgot, we would look back and chuckle when we realized the oversight. Few folks would ever imagine that a couple as emotionally intimate as we would forget important days.

We laughed and said it was because we treat every day like a wedding anniversary.

CHAPTER 7

Living the Dream

MOST OF THE TIME life does not measure up to our ideals. But all modesty aside, Spurgeon and I were dynamic together! God showered us with success in our relationship, finances, friendships, church, neighborhood, health, and everything.

Spurge's first bass fish out of our one-acre pond

There is a passage in Joel 2:25 (ESV) that says, "I will restore to you what the swarming locusts have eaten." And that is exactly what He did! My Spanish came in handy for teaching school and junior college in a bilingual setting. Spurgeon's limited Japanese proved useful on numerous occasions. We formed a couple of short-term mission teams to serve in Peru that were adventurous and helpful. We implemented our bicultural qualities to serve the community and the world.

Yup, we felt the success of those years when the damage the locusts cost us was, indeed, redeemed.

By grace and power, after five years of hard work and fabulous togetherness, we sold our beautifully rehabbed Chicago two-story brick and traded it for an old ranch house on a twenty-acre farm in Southwest Michigan. Locals refer to the area as Michiana because it shares a border, and similar weather, with Indiana.

We had made a list of criteria that we shared with the realtors: twenty-plus acres, preferably a stately old brick home, way off the road, with wood-burning fireplace and water in the form of a creek, pond, or lake. We casually looked for homes and camped for two years all around SW Michigan, but not one met our list of criteria. Nothing came remotely close. We saw twenty-seven houses and bought the last one we looked at.

When we did finally find our dream home, we knew it immediately, like love at first sight. It was a city block off the road and had a one-acre pond that was teaming with bass! The pond was in the back yard, but the surrounding turf was so overgrown you couldn't walk around it. The yard was messy, full of half-burnt piles of garbage and accumulations of junk. The small cow barn was half-high with straw and manure. The ample, three-bedroom, 1959 ranch house offered a fine living room fireplace. The place was all in good repair, except it was in great need of decorating and grooming.

The distribution of land was fabulous. There was about one-third tillable, one-third forest, and one-third swamp. Before this, we would have thought of that much swampland as undesirable. But this bog hosted a huge variety of flora and fauna that we noticed even on our initial visit with the realtor. We heard Sandhill cranes, spotted white-tailed deer, blue heron, beaver dams, and even a mink! All of this inside of a one-hour visit!

Well, this little spot of paradise was everything we wanted, with the exception of it not being made of brick, nor was it historical. After praying excitedly about it, we waited a week to be sure, and then bought the twenty-acre parcel.

We pulled seven standard truckloads of junk out of the house, garage, outbuildings, and yard. But the bones of the house were perfect, as was the setting, and this was to be our home for the next twenty-four years! We moved two years after this fine purchase was made.

A helpful caravan of people drove to Michigan to facilitate our move. Brothers, sisters, kids, and neighbors helped us load up the moving van from our Chicago home. Our friend next door said he had to be crazy to help his two favorite neighbors move out of state. Spurgeon's sister, Georgia, told me if I went to one more garage sale, she would never help us move again. I made no vows.

Arriving at the farm two-and-a-half hours after leaving our newly sold Chicago home, everything went slick as a whistle. I had moved many times in my life and was good at it. All boxes were packed safely with labels and numbers as to what room they should go into. We had the bedrooms numbered as well as the boxes, so all articles went to the right spot. I packed the box of bed and bath linens in the car with me but had the beds put into the moving van last. That way, they would be out first. I directed traffic as people brought boxes into the house. Spurgeon's daughter, Linda, who was with the linens, made up the beds as quickly as they were assembled. It all went so smoothly, that we sat up and snacked, laughed, and played cards till we all crashed.

We spent the first night in our new, country home.

We had officially retired! He was 59 and I, 42. We both had fabulous health. We ate nutritiously. I wanted to keep it that way, to be certain Spurgeon stayed in tip-top health. The world was our oyster!

The Underground Railroad went through this area, and because during abolitionist time local Quakers housed and helped provide land for incoming freedom seekers (formerly referred to as runaway slaves), some stayed. As a result, the immediate area is very racially mixed. We found that, in itself, to be an enticement.

An amusing story floats around our neck of the woods. A friend of mine told it to me. It took place at a large luncheon of church ladies preceding a Bible study, which included a healthy pallet of ethnic mixes. Well into the luncheon, in the midst of a conversation concerning races, a young woman blurted out, "I don't believe in Blacks and Whites marrying each other. The Bible says, 'There shall be no mixing of the races!'"

My friend said the statement met with a profound hush.

Then, a little elder with a firm voice broke the silence: "Giiirrrl! You'd better shut yo' mouth and open yo' Bible!" My friend added that a round of prolonged, stifled chuckles followed.

Becoming part of a church was one of our priorities. We used the same method of finding one that we used in Chicago. They say the best restaurants and churches are both found by word of mouth. So when we met churchgoers, we would ask where they went, as we were looking for a home church.

It is interesting that we received nearly the identical response from people, city or country. When we revealed that we were looking for a place of worship, many got wide-eyed and said something stupid like, "Oh, we are a Bible-believing church. It says in the Old Testament that there should be no mixing of the races. And we follow that tenet."

Well, anyone who interprets the Bible to be separatist and select has not understood that God told the Israelites not to marry outside of their "race" because they were the "chosen people," and He didn't want them to be saddled with *unbelievers*. It would weaken their faith. In the New Testament "there is neither Jew nor Greek, slave nor free, male nor female." (Galatians 3:28, BSB) We all have equal access to God through Christ. Differences are null and void.

In the lengthy search for a good house of worship, we met a neighbor who invited us to his church. We went on the upcoming Sunday, but the pastor was out of town. So, he came over to meet us on his return.

Pastor Sam, half my age and one third of Spurgeon's, knocked on the door at (nearly) nine o'clock on a summer night. Replacing the wooden floor in our guest bath, we were up to our eyeballs in dirt and glue.

I answered the door, found out who it was, and hesitantly asked the pleasant-looking young man to enter. I motioned for Sam to be seated. When I headed toward the bathroom to alert Spurgeon as to the pastor's presence, Sam followed me into the living room and bath, where Spurgeon was on his knees. Spurgeon remained there until he could afford a break from the glue project. Then he and I sat at the kitchen table, nodding for Sam to do the same.

The next thing Spurgeon did shocked me! I didn't know if he was slightly irritated at having an interruption, or if he was attempting, in his fatigue, to be funny. Or maybe this was a test of some type.

"You want a beer?" Spurgeon asked bluntly. A beer! What in the world was he talking about? He didn't even drink beer! And there assuredly was none in the house! Was he testing the young pastor? What would he do if the guy said yes?"

"No, thanks. I was just excited to come and meet you two," responded Sam.

He left shortly before midnight.

We found out afterwards that on returning home, his wife, Pam, asked, "Where have you been so late?"

"At the new couple's house, Spurgeon and Deb's."

"This late? Sam!"

"You have to meet them to understand, Sweetheart."

And meet we did. We slipped like magnets toward each other: Fast friends, confidants, traveling companions, you name it. Our ages were vastly different, but we shared the same hearts and goals. We all wanted to be more like Jesus.

Additionally, many jobs out in the country require more than one man. If Spurgie shoveled a truck load of manure, cleaned the guts from a deer, or built a shed or porch, the young, energetic Sam was there, ready to get his hands dirty.

Now that we had a church, it was time to buy an ATV! We decided to get the all-terrain vehicle to help with farm work and gather and move firewood. I must admit that it was I who initially wanted the four-wheeler, and I wanted it far more for play than work.

The day we purchased our joy buggy, we were anxious to try it out. Not sure about the road rules in Michigan concerning ATVs, we decided to wait until midnight and then run around the hood. That way we would encounter few vehicles and hopefully, no sheriff.

The night air teased our nostrils as they drew in the fragrance of fields, green and lush. The navy sky was strewn with masses of stars. The temperature was ideal. The invigorating country air refreshed us and cleaned out the cobwebs in our brains.

We covered twenty miles before reaching home, and we never once saw a vehicle. We felt freer than we'd ever felt and praised God for the privilege and pleasure of living in His glorious creation.

Speaking later with our chief of police, we learned that rules for ATVs vary township to township. In our county, we are not supposed to drive on state roads nor busy roads nor in town. Helmets are mandatory by all riders at all times.

So, it turned out we were purely legal on our joy ride, which made us happy.

Oh, right, I forgot. The law says no one should ride double. We faltered in that regard.

Four wheelers are such well-built machines. They seldom break down and they last forever. It took us twenty years of hauling wood and driving difficult terrain to wear out our first four-wheeler. We are on our second now. It has a 500 cubic centimeter engine with a two- or four-wheel-drive interchange. Very versatile.

What privilege we Americans live with! So much choice, so much beauty! I was living my personal dream: The most wonderful, handsome Christian man in the world loved me, we had a dog and an ATV and lived in the country near water. That is my happy spot.

[For creative ideas on ministry possibilities, look at CHAPTER 17 and see how an ATV may be used as a healthy, healing opportunity.]

CHAPTER 8

Learning to be Country Again

OUR HOUSEHOLD GREW AND shrank and grew again over the years. Nephews came for the summer to do country stuff, and grandkids left the confines of Chicago to spend summers in Michigan. Sometimes the grandkids rode out a full year's stay along with homeschooling, which they truly wanted to experience and enjoyed tremendously. We had perpetual visitors looking to retreat from life in the big city (including former students from the Chicago public school system), and later we added a Peruvian son to the family. The house flowed with guests and family, fluctuating like waves.

But there was a learning curve to living a true country lifestyle. Our first big lesson was when Spurgeon bought a tractor and plowed the front acreage for the first time.

As he rounded the bend of the field, which was half complete, a pickup truck rolled up and waited at the neck of the driveway. Ultimately, Spurgie drove in that direction and paused to address the gentleman, who appeared to want to speak with my tractor-drivin' hubby.

"Son, you are trying. But you sure ain't no farmer!" stated our wrinkled visitor with the visor cap and farmer's tan.

And that is how we met one of our elderly neighbors, who was tickled to tell the inquiring newbie how to rightfully plow a field.

I'm guessing you'd seldom have to worry about a man who starts a conversation with, "Son . . . "

Another neighbor got a real kick out of us when we asked him if we could have the willow tree the county cut down on the edge of his property. Attempting to stifle a smile, he said, "Sure!"

Little did we know that willow is not a hardwood and it flash burns. It's a heap of ashes in a minute with little sustainable heat. It's like a burp in the wind.

But it only took us once to learn. Once burnt, twice shy. (Literally.)

In the vegetable garden we learned about liming a field to acquire the proper acid balance. The produce was so much happier!

When we tore down our friend's 150-year-old barn to repurpose the lumber, we found out those one-and-a-half-century-old wooden planks had started to petrify!

Well, maybe not petrify, but harden, for sure. The norm is, it takes my guy two or three whacks to pound a standard-sized construction nail into a board. The vintage barn board was taking seven to nine strikes for the best of them! Per nail!

We learned that this area, like all glacial states, has a high quantity of fieldstone. I was young and strong and had a four-wheeler, and did I go to town with the rocks! One day Pam, the young pastor's wife, and I went out and scrounged gorgeous mini boulders for our yards. We both felt a bit like Wonder Woman by the time we finished. Sam said Pam and I ruined the transmission on their vehicle with an overload of rocks in their trunk. We told the guys next time we went rock hunting they could go with us. If they were to lift the big boys, we would not bust the weight limit!

We learned that blue racer snakes, like the one under our chicken coop, are six feet or more in length and are fast, moving up to four miles an hour. It is a non-venomous critter, has a gorgeous iridescent-blue coat, and prefers to run rather than strike.

I also learned red meat bullheads are terrible tasting. But in this area, we have white meat bullheads, and they are absolutely delectable!

Visitors to our one-acre pond taught us that what is fun in practice may not always be beneficial. When we fed our fish in the evenings, we also enjoyed numerous snapping turtles of all sizes that came to feed. We enjoyed them until we realized that they were eating our fingerling fish! We then started eating snappers, when in hunting season.

Mel, our life-long Michigan resident and friend, taught us that the Sandhill crane (a pair resided in our swamp) was nearly wiped out during the depression. This is because they are slow moving and easily captured. They are also delicious. Their population has now recovered.

A stunning couple of American bitterns showed up at our pond for a summer and nearly annihilated the frog and snake population. Their tall, lime-green legs identified them easily. After a summer of gorging and reproducing three fledglings, they moved on to greener pastures.

In our small town, we experienced a giant shift in business practices regarding check writing and the need for personal identification. In the city, no business will take a private check unless you have two pieces of credentials and one with a picture. In the country we asked the feed mill, after purchasing about $200 in seed, if they would like to see our drivers' license with the check. The clerk gave a little smirk and wink. "Nah. We know where you live. And, what's more, we know what you are doing!"

With all of this learning going on there was never a dull moment.

I wanted us to stay healthy forever so we could always do fun stuff like planting a field of alfalfa.

One day, Spurgeon hadn't taken his vitamins and herbs. When reminded, he responded, "Oh, not to worry. I want to do everything I can to be around as long as possible. I like being your husband!"

I really enjoyed those love reinforcements. I may possibly be needier than the average female in regard to affection, but I ate up all his touching attentions, verbal or physical. Give me togetherness and sweet nothings in my ear over presents any day. That is my love language.

Couples at church decided to study Gary Chapman's *The Five Love Languages*. One of the younger girls, Sally, (whom I would claim as a daughter in a hot minute) agreed with Spurgeon and me that sincere, loving words are our most precious and appreciated gifts.

Ruth, a treasured girl who grew up thinking of us as grandparents, was recently married and was taking the love languages course with us. She boldly stated one evening, "I'm going to handle the gift issue like Deb does."

Spurgeon and his young buddy, Ruth

Curious, Sally asked, "And just how is that?"

Ruth enlightened us with her insights. "Oh, she tells Spurgeon, 'No, I can't think of a thing I want for my birthday.'"

"Or," continued Ruth, "'No, please don't buy me anything. I have no needs.'"

"Then, when she really wants something, she goes big time!" Here Ruthie's eyes widen for effect, and she mocks, "'Yah, I really would like a four wheeler.'"

"Or, 'Well, you could build me a 12 x 36 deck off the north side of the house.'"

"Or," the teaser continued, "'Isn't it about time we went to the Big Apple for fun and food?'"

"She gets whatever she wants!" Ruth smiled.

Very observant on her part.

By this time in our marriage, I realized that this was one dynamic man of God, who lived his faith daily and got, generally, what he wanted. Also, because he was so darn amiable it was hard to not comply with him.

Initially, I thought it might be only my biased viewpoint of him that made him appear so outrageously, magnetically charming. Then I started observing people's reactions to Spurgeon.

For example, after work one day, back in the city, Spurgeon and I walked our favorite city haunt, the sparsely populated Japanese Garden just behind the Museum of Science and Industry in Chicago. It was our way of getting away without leaving Chi town. As we circled the huge pond, we encountered a former neighbor of Spurgeon's. The two men threw their arms around each other, diving into a jovial conversation about the old hood. On parting, the friend said, "Bye guy. Love you till I die!"

I tenderly adopted that phrase for my beloved family and friends.

There, at the Japanese Garden, we decided to sit in the lonely parking lot overlooking the giant pond reflecting evening streetlights. As we sat smooching and talking, another vehicle rolled up and parked next to us. We thought it a bit odd, since the parking lot was empty.

However, as soon as the stranger pulled up, he rolled down all his windows, whipped out his alto saxophone and began romancing us! He wasn't John Coltrane, but his tunes tickled our senses. We sat in the car curled up with each other, smooching only a polite amount, while absorbing the combination of romantic and Christian jazz. We couldn't have picked a better way to culminate a day filled with God's presence and love.

As we prepared to leave this amorous setting, since we had work the next day, we thanked the talented stranger. He nodded and smiled. "The pleasure is all mine. I had hoped to play for someone who would appreciate the tunes."

How wonderful he encountered us! We found romance to be magnetic.

At home there were six women who would call Spurgeon and say to me, "Yeah, tell him his favorite niece is calling." (You know who you are Fanny, Rosie, Sonia, Venicia, Andrea, and Giesela.) Then his "favorite nephew" would start calling, in multiples.

Pam, our pastor's wife, said she never met anyone who possessed *all* the gifts of the Spirit like Spurgeon. That, too, was a gift to me.

Our girlfriend and fellow congregant, Sally, said he was one of the few men she knew who treats his wife as Christ treats His bride, the Church. Precious, precious are words of gold.

Amazingly, no matter how complimented Spurgeon was, his ego never inflated. He was beautifully humble.

Billy Sunday said, "Your reputation is what people say about you. Your character is what God and your wife know about you." This is from www.azquotes.com; TOP 25 QUOTES BY BILLY SUNDAY.

So, as his wife, I can safely say that Spurgeon was a humble man.

And what, you may ask, does it feel like to be in love with a complete man of God?

It feels safe. It feels like a warm bed with mounds of quilts on a Minnesota winter's night.

It feels empowering. A *real* man makes a woman feel she can truly face the cruelties of the world and, by God's grace, do something about them.

It feels like every day is an opportunity to make a difference. At least in the life and wellbeing of that stunning face that smiles and winks over the breakfast table!

It felt solid, dependable, and true.

It felt a lot like my relationship with God.

About the time that we got settled in our retirement, Paul and Marty, my missionary friends in Peru, began seeking people interested in forming short-term mission trips to help build a variety of orphanages in their beloved country. For a combination of cultural reasons, there were many young boys on the streets. The idea was to get sixteen people together who would act and travel as a team and lend their time, talents, and treasures to accomplish the building of units. Each team would spend two weeks, working with the materials they bought with money they donated. Room, board, and in-country transport was all prearranged. The hosts even organized adventures during the stay, as this is a fascinating country with spectacular geography and history.

Teams from all over the world came to honor the ongoing, hard work of this dedicated couple.

Getting to work each morning

Making mud and straw bricks just like 2,000 years ago

We formed two different teams two different years. We sought out friends, family, and strangers to fill the positions. By God's grace, we compiled sixteen generous people who wanted to go. Our job as coaches was now to 1) Make a timeline, for distribution, of all that must be done prior to the trip. 2) Have multiple meetings to establish camaraderie and pass out prayer lists. 3) Arrange fundraisers and see them through. 4) Start making travel arrangements for the whole group.

This is an oversimplification, but it gives the reader an idea of the involvement.

Initially, we started this without the help of our church. Later, the church wanted to help, so we agreed to that. Prayer support was vital and a fund was started to help defray the substantial cost for the short-term missionaries.

We were excited for this adventure and began asking everyone within our reach. We asked neighbors, friends, acquaintances, and strangers.

In a meeting one day with our pastor (not Sam, who had moved), he stated that all the mission candidates must be Christians. We had never been of that conviction.

We politely disagreed. Long-term missionaries most certainly need a calling and commitment to Christ. But this was a costly two-week adventure. We needed willing laborers with good hearts, who wanted to put out hard-earned money to help make the world a little better place for some kids. If these volunteers wanted to help, and found adventure along the way, we were willing to have them on board. That they loved the Lord or would, by osmosis, learn about Him, was good enough for us. That they threw in their greenbacks to advance the cause of Christ, knowingly or unknowingly, meant their hearts were in the right place, no matter their belief or unbelief. We insisted on an open policy in this regard.

This presented a conflict.

Since we were not willing to bend in this matter, my elder prayer partner, Alice, a founder of the church, intervened. (She is the wife of the man who asked us to this church.) Ultimately, the church board worked it out and *all* candidates passed with flying colors.

Each time we went on a mission trip to Peru or to aid in the Katrina crisis, lives of our team members were forever changed. God uses willing people with generous hearts. His face was shining down on us!

See more work-related photos in Chapter 17, "Fun Stuff."

A social worker, named Ruth, confirmed that we did have it pretty-well-altogether. She interviewed us as part of the process of adopting a child from Peru. She spent two hours at the initial appointment with both of us, followed by two hours with each of us individually, then a two-hour summary. When (and if) the child came, we would need a two-hour final home visit and evaluation.

That came to fruition when she met our new son, Yermalay (pronounced Ger-ma-lie), for a visit in our home. When all was said and done, Ruth confessed to us, "On our initial meeting, I looked at the two of you and wondered what in the world you had in common. You are from totally opposite climates and cultures and from two different time eras. Your educational trainings were in diverse corners. I seriously wondered what you had in common. However, after my full study I found that you share a tremendous amount, including faith, common values, mutual goals and interests, and a true enjoyment of each other. You are far more alike than you are different!"

We pretty much knew that, but it was rewarding to hear it from a trained professional, whose job it was to evaluate couples.

Yermalay Johnathan Wiggins, born in the Amazonian region of Peru, was now our son. Our friends called us "The Rainbow Family." The vast cultural exchanges enriched our lives and expanded our intellect.

And now we had delectable Peruvian cuisine to add to our menu!

It's a boy!

Even in parenting, Spurgeon seemed flawless. At times, it was disconcerting to live with someone who never did anything objectionable.

I believe myself no less dedicated to God than Spurgeon, but I am a far more fallible person than he, and obviously less mature. I tend to be a creative thinker with a great deal of spontaneity, balanced with good follow-through. Spurgeon is the rock-solid kind of guy that thinks everything out before stepping forward. He tends to make fewer mistakes than I. Together; we made the most perfect team that totally balanced one another.

Oddly enough, after a while, seeing the room light up with his presence began to bother me. Soon I figured out that I was jealous of his character. Shame, shame on me. It is *not* okay to be jealous of your husband because he possesses so many great traits!

Spurgeon was the best thing that ever happened to me in my entire life and now I was objecting to that gift?

God responded with, "Be transformed by the renewing of your mind." (Romans 12:2, NIV)

Yes. Please. I asked Him for a blank page on my heart so that He would impress those words indelibly.

I adopted many of Spurgie's traits by way of osmosis.

And God changed me because it was His pleasure and because He says in Romans chapter twelve that we should be transformed.

Daily diving into the *Word* for family devotions, we enjoyed a constant diet of *The Upper Room,* a long-standing devotional to help the reader understand practical applications of the scriptures. We not only used it as a couple's devotional but invited whoever was staying with us to partake of the growth experience. People really enjoy the stimulating discussions!

One day we were reading Proverbs' (Chapter 31, NIV) description of a "wife of noble character." In public discussions, I found many people are not acquainted with this ideal. And the implications are fascinating to imagine in regard to life in the twenty first century. I have printed it here for the sake of reflection and discussion.

The Wife of Noble Character

10. A wife of noble character who can find?
    She is worth far more than rubies.
11. Her husband has full confidence in her
    and lacks nothing of value.
12. She brings him good, not harm,
    all the days of her life.
13. She selects wool and flax
    and works with eager hands.

14. She is like the merchant ships,
    bringing her food from afar.
15. She gets up while it is still night;
    she provides food for her family
    and portions for her female servants.
16. She considers a field and buys it;
    out of her earnings she plants a vineyard.
17. She sets about her work vigorously;
    her arms are strong for her tasks.
18. She sees that her trading is profitable,
    and her lamp does not go out at night.
19. In her hand she holds the distaff
    and grasps the spindle with her fingers.
20. She opens her arms to the poor
    and extends her hands to the needy.
21. When it snows, she has no fear for her household;
    for all of them are clothed in scarlet.
22. She makes coverings for her bed;
    she is clothed in fine linen and purple.
23. Her husband is respected at the city gate,
    where he takes his seat among the elders of the land.
24. She makes linen garments and sells them,
    and supplies the merchants with sashes.
25. She is clothed with strength and dignity;
    she can laugh at the days to come.
26. She speaks with wisdom,
    and faithful instruction is on her tongue.
27. She watches over the affairs of her household
    and does not eat the bread of idleness.
28. Her children arise and call her blessed;
    her husband also, and he praises her.

We finished our reading and discussion of the marvelous virtues of a good wife. Spurgeon gazed across the table at me with those luscious, deep eyes, and with his irrepressible smile he said, "You are that noble woman, *Amor*. You do all of those things except get up early."

In humility, praying that he was spot on, I leaned into him, chuckled, and reminded him that he was the one who first started sleeping in, and he had requested a bedfellow!

It is true, in our waning years, we did enjoy the luxury of sleeping in and we loved every minute of it!

There was a *déjà vu* experience that ultimately brought us a great deal of comfort, adding validity to our already firm belief we were meant for each other.

In college in the late '60s my roommate, Marlene, listened to a strange, outstanding dream of mine. In the vision I saw myself in a country kitchen with lots of red and white. I was serving a Black male and a Latin boy waffles for breakfast. The dream made it obvious to me that this was my husband and son.

The reason I found this to be bizarre is that, at the time, I had not met but one Black man in my entire life. He was an acquaintance who attended Trinity College with me. And I knew zero Latin males.

That dream, and what it divulged, was completely erased from my memory until it came to fruition thirty years later!

As I walked those waffles to my hubby and son in that red and white country kitchen, a stark recollection flashed before me that I had been in that exact spot decades earlier in my dream in college. Call it a time warp, stepping back (or forward) in time, or *déjà vu*. Call it anything you want. I had seen the future. Then, I unwittingly lived it.

If it is meant to be, it will happen.

CHAPTER 9

Those Are Some Fascinating ISMS!

I HAVE COMPOSED A list of Spurgeonisms over the years that will demonstrate his humility, humor, and wisdom. For a time, I wondered how he could come up with such simple, yet profound thoughts. Only much later did I realize that these are (mostly) cultural quips that are common amongst Black Americans. But to this Minnesotan, they were innovative mentality.

1. "God don't like ugly!" This was said to any of our grandkids or son when they displayed an inappropriate and unpleasant attitude. It produced nearly magical results, making the recipients think about and alter their behavior. I highly recommend it as a household management tactic and personal checkpoint.

2. "Ain't nothin' 'bout him (her) that a little bit of Jesus wouldn't help." Prior to his saying that, I was thinking mean thoughts toward the person that had just wronged us. Hearing him express that idea put me to shame. I bowed my head.

3. "Ain't no one monkey stop no show." Spurgeon said this to me on an occasion when we had organized a fundraiser, and someone did

not hold up her end of the bargain. I was discouraged. In the end, all went well and Good was served . . . And Spurgeon was right.

4. "He weren't worth two dead flies." I heard this applied to only one person. Now, this one shocked me, coming out of the mouth of my gentle husband!

"*Amor* [we used the Spanish version of this endearment], how could you say that about anybody? That is absolutely terrible!"

Turned out that this man of whom he spoke had stated, "Work is for mules and fools, and I ain't neither." He mooched constantly, and fondled peoples' trousers on approach to see if they had money. I asked Spurgeon about the "Nothing wrong with him that a little bit of Jesus wouldn't help" mentality. He stated simply and sadly, "The fear of God is the beginning of wisdom, and he passed up God his whole life." This came from the mouth of a man who rarely had harsh statements for anyone.

5. "My Mama told me that God gave us all twenty-four hours a day to mind our own business and twenty-four hours a day to stay out of our neighbors'."

6. "Mama always said there's more room out than there is in." This was stated in times where a burp or gas escaped the body. Fannie Wiggins was my kind of practical woman.

7. "My Mama use to refer to men who don't take care of business as 'Breath in britches.'" That one took me a while. It seemed like a euphemism. I wondered why she didn't just say he was a useless jerk and get it over with. I asked our niece, Fannie, why she put it so poetically. I loved her response. "A trouser (britches) is an inanimate object that has no purpose but to cover something. Instead of being unkind and say the person was worthless, she said something that is understood." What forethought and restraint! I think I'll try that also!

The wise Fannie Wiggins, Spurgeon's Mother

8. "You live till you die." Oh, my, how I objected to and rejected this one when he first used it on me. I was thinking of doing something that was not in the best interest of my health. And he had the audacity to say "You live till you die; you know," on me! My retort? "That's stupid! So obvious. Like I don't know that! What's your point?"

He never answered. He just gave me *the look*. All his kids, relatives and friends know what *the look* is. He lowers his head in silence, raises his brows, purses his lips ever-so-slightly, cocks his lowered face slightly to the left (he was ambidextrous on many occasions) and made a barely audible "phhhhh." This was sometimes accompanied by a slight shrug of the shoulder. The gesture results in an effective manner of coercion, should you want to try it.

9. "You've got my nose wide open!" Say what? Is that good? What in the world does that mean? Well, it means that the person has the hots for you. It is actually based on scientific fact. When many species of animals, humans included, find a member of the opposite sex extremely attractive, their pupils dilate and their nose flares up, "wide open." I am not joking! Whenever he spoke, "You've got my nose wide open, girl," it slipped out of his mouth smooth as silk. Instead of it being humorous it was alluring!

Mississippi Meets Minnesota

10. "He's smelling himself." This is commonly used to describe kids when they become teens and suddenly know everything about everything, and you can't tell them anything.

11. "Always ask, Deb. They can only say yes, or no, or hell no! But always ask."

This was particularly important for me to hear, because one of our God-given jobs was to raise funds for charitable causes. It entails doing a lot of *the ask*, a job which often makes me uneasy. Fortunately, Americans are generous people, so we received a lot more yeses than noes, and only one "Hell no!"

12. "You can't get mad at her. You already know she's short." I'll leave that one alone.

13. When I contemplated a purchase I wasn't certain about, he might check me with these questions: "Did you live without it yesterday?"

"Yes."

Continuing the inquisition: "Did you live without it today?"

"Yes," I replied with a bit of suspicion.

"Then you can live without it tomorrow." Now, many of you who actually enjoy shopping may think this is a form of control. (I find little pleasure in shopping.) But we had a pretty good grip on how *not* to spend money. It wasn't that he challenged me because of the money, rather because of the American habit of materialism. I have, in turn, asked those same questions to myself and to girlfriends who also found the thought process helpful.

14. "I don't have a personal heaven or hell to put anyone in." This has always topped my list of favorites. It is so easy for humans to be judgmental. If we focus on a picture of that statement in our minds and apply it to our temptations to judge, we are more likely to resist that sin.

15. After touching a tender spot and hearing me cry out, Spurgie flinched and retorted, "Oh, no! I can't hurt you! That hurts me!" Such

a sensitive thing for a spouse to say. He spoke these words with gentleness and a light kiss.

Now, I can't pass up this opportunity to share, alongside the Spurgeonisms, the Minnesotanisms that stemmed from my being born and raised in a state with a huge Scandinavian influence.

1. *Uffda!* was my Nordic answer to many a happening. Something fell and made a mess, *"Uffda!"* On falling ill, I groaned *"Uffda. I feel yucky."*

Spurgie was puzzled. "I can't get a grasp of your *'Uffda.'* You use it as a response to a variety of circumstances. What does it mean?"

I'd never been asked to define the word before. In Minnesota, its ubiquitous presence needs no interpretation. Defining it is like putting a gate around air. *"Uffda,"* [spelling may vary], is a Scando expression used as an interjection. One may express dismay or annoyance with the word, as to say, "*'Uffda,* that stinks!"

But it may also be used empathetically, in order to express compassion; "*Uffda,* that must hurt!"

With that kind of range, the word is versatile! From then on it was fun to watch *'uffda'* form and vocalize on the lovely lips of my handsome Black husband. My superior at Southwestern Michigan College, where I taught as an adjunct professor in a bilingual position, said the same thing about me when I spoke in Spanish. "It is captivating to see Spanish come out of the mouth of someone who looks so Nordic!" Languages are just plain fun.

2. "By golly" is an old-fashioned expression that may not be unique to Minnesota, but I like the way the oldsters, like Uncle Andrew, born in Norway, said it: "By degollus!" These words are used to express surprise or delight. One summer my brother, Roy, his dad, Andrew, and I were running errands. Uncle Andrew exclaimed, "By degollus, the kids are out of school early today."

We were on country roads and a fully loaded hay wagon was in front of us. Roy asked, "Why do you say that, Dad?"

"Well, because there's the school bus and it's only noon," observed my uncle.

"By degollus, Uncle Andrew, I think you need your glasses changed!" I suggested.

Both Spurgie and I enjoyed using this expression and played with it as yet another cultural exchange, often with a chuckle.

What I found to be endearing was the absolute delight that Spurgeon took in my Minnesota heritage and Scandinavian humor. When we visited home, or we traveled and encountered fellow Minnesotans, he fixated on our cultural exchanges, specifically the Ole and Lena jokes, always accompanied by a heavy Scando brogue. Spurgie would smile broadly; "Oh boy, here comes the Ole and Lena jokes! We'll be hearing them every day we camp here!"

And so, Minnesotans and Mississippians sat around the campfire sharing the latest in the popular cultural jokes, always told with the Scando brogue. Generally, Norwegians told jokes to make Swedes look stupid. Swedes told the same jokes and turned them around to make Norwegians look stupid. If you were a mixed Norski and Swede breed, you picked the Danes, Fins, or Icelanders to look dumb. The exchanges are hilarious, and I would like you to experience this Midwest cultural icon, so I have included a film of one of the jokes in the last chapter, "Fun Stuff."

Spurgeon jumped with both feet into the jokes. He often insisted that I tell them, then sat back and thoroughly enjoyed the telling or retelling! An admirable, chameleon character, he would have made a great Viking.

But, *uffda,* he had a crumby, fake, Norski brogue!

CHAPTER 10

And All That Jazz

THE MOST FASCINATING CULTURAL acquisition for me in our marriage was the falling in love with and owning of jazz. I had no idea that this field of music was so captivating. It incorporates everything from history to humor, romance to revolution.

After being musically deprived for a number of years via extensive travel and remote settings, one of my first requests on my return to the city was that I go to a Judds' concert. This was back when Wynona Judd and her two daughters were touring together. Fully aware that country music was not at the top of Spurgeon's list of easy listening music, I meekly asked him if he would go to the concert with me.

"Absolutely! When? Where?" He responded in a snap with a smile.

At home after the concert, sitting with a raspberry tea (our favorite), I asked him about his willingness to not only go to the concert but the appearance that he enjoyed it. I admired his open mind in examining a type of beauty with which he was not familiar.

His response was immediate and touching. "Well, I figured if I went with you, at least I would come home with a better understanding of why you like country music and maybe glean some liking for it myself."

Wow! It appeared I would be learning a lot from this outstanding new husband. That Spurgeon went to country music concerts, and then turned around to introduce me to jazz appreciation, added a whole new dimension to my listening engagements. The grasp of jazz gave me a whole new insight into subcultures and history. How colorful was that learning!

It is difficult for me to understand how certain genres of music are considered to be acceptable church music and other forms are considered unsuitable. If the tune is gorgeous and the thoughts of a song are acceptable to God, then why would that same music not be acceptable to the church?

I know Sam Lavine can rock the steeples with his saxophone worship, *Friend of God,* and God loves every note of it! I have heard jazz praise songs that would knock your socks off. (Since God is not surprised at anything, that does not hold true for Him!) And I've heard other tunes that compelled me to bended knee.

Little did I know the variety and intrigue of this genre of music. The Black American culture has invented a wide range of fascinating musical categories such as spirituals, jazz, hip-hop, blues, and rap. Spurgeon's considerable knowledge of jazz came from living history. He lived with juke joints, and early radio. He sat on a porch after church in Indianola, Mississippi listening to B.B. King stroking his guitar named Lucille. Spurgie knew the names and words of more songs than I knew existed. He said he had often wanted to play a guitar and sing, but his early onset of a hearing deficit (caused by industrial pollution) robbed him of that desire.

We found a wonderful enlightenment through the tape series, "The History of Jazz," by the premier trumpet performer and historian, Winton Marcellus. Through him, we encountered a most usable idea. He said good jazz is like a good argument. Each instrument, like each person, expresses his or her point of view in his or her own way, making bold statements as to the person's identity. When every instrument (person) has expressed himself or herself thoroughly, they then come together corporately to make beautiful harmony.

We ate up that philosophy. We applied this mentality to discussions and taught it to others.

For dancing and romancing at home, Spurgeon chose Nat King Cole over anyone. "When I Fall in Love," was his favorite.

My categorical choice is the smooth groove of Kevin Mahogany and his *You've Got What it Takes* album. Each time that tune played, Spurgeon turned to me with a gorgeous smile and raised eyebrows. He pointed at me, nodding his head. And silly me, I melted even at the anticipation of him doing that. Play Kevin Mahogany again, with purpose! Love is so crazy. It's a little bit of heaven on earth.

One day, Spurgeon popped an amusing, early morning question on me, just as I was leaving for work. Tugging my coat sleeve, he gently pulled me back into the apartment and purred in my ear, "Is you my Baby? Or ain't you my Baby"

"I is!" was my delighted, giggly response. He gave me a quick kiss and off I went. I learned that evening that his amusing question stemmed from a song title popularly performed by Louis Jordan.

If someone won a board game and we wanted to teasingly shame the winner, we would join in an [altered] Fats Waller statement: "I don't like you cause your feets too big!" So if you want a good laugh, find and listen to the hilarious song, "Your Feets Too Big."

We all guffawed when we played Louis Jordan's "Five Guys Named Mo," for our Pastor Mo. He laughed and put his first foot forward into the world of jazz.

For those who appreciate imagination and creativity, follow the scat singers. They take their voices and make them sound like musical instruments. Those famous for their wonderful scat are Louis Armstrong, Ella Fitzgerald, Scatman Crothers, and Tony Bennett. For those who really like the queen of scat, watch the documentary called "Ella" that is riddled with fascinating, melodic history.

Jazz musicians often express personal philosophies through their song. I pondered Louie Armstrong and Louis Jordan's duet, "Life is So Peculiar," and found profundity in the midst of simplicity. It reminds me of the Biblical proverb, "there's nothing new under the sun." (Ecclesiastes 1:9, NIV)

Since two people sing this version of "Life is So Peculiar," it is termed a "duet." But, at nearly no point do the two men sing simultaneously. It is more likely that one singer makes a statement, and the second singer replies to that statement. Plus, they do my favorite trick and add aspects of scat, mixed with humor. It is a tune well worth your while to hear. When you do listen, you can ask yourself if it was ridiculously simplistic, or profound? You decide. . . .

Spurgeon had a handle on discussions concerning jazz. I had the handle on art forms, especially mixed media. More than once, in social groups, we discussed an age-old debate: Does our culture produce art through individual contributions and observations, or does our art produce our culture?

In the case of "Strange Fruit," first performed by Billie Holiday in 1939, the song was a reaction to the vigilante hangings (and burnings) of Black Americans all over the United States for centuries. Interestingly, a New York Jewish teacher named Abel Meeropol wrote the impacting words, first as a poem, and then he later reformed it as a song. I gleaned some of that information from a computer article entitled "The Pop History Dig."

In the tune, Holiday mourns that Southern arbors are adorned with an odd fruit that has bug-eyes, charred torsos, and is meat for the carrion fowl. One of the lines references the stench of combustible bodies. This line grabs my olfactory nerves immediately. I have had the misfortune of smelling burning flesh. It is an odor that haunts the brain's memory for a lifetime.

It is a stark and abrasive description of public and vigilante hangings. Though the numbers of hangings are impossible to record (there are huge discrepancies in the tallies), the act is despicable and fosters cruelty. It was sadly repulsive and sick to see, as one investigates the topic of death via a rope and tree, the gleeful faces of the onlookers in historical photos where whole towns came out. The onlookers had the coldness of heart to bring children to these horrifying public events. The innocents witnessed the excruciating deaths of (often innocent) victims. Of the thousands of recorded deaths in our country, the vast majority were executed in three Southern states. Georgia, Mississippi, and Texas have the dubious distinction of public hangings by the hundreds. Seventy two percent of the hangings were perpetuated against Black people, according to an NAACP investigation.

The 1930s and '40s saw art forms respond in protest against this cruel killing form. Ida B. Wells, the NAACP, a group of female journalists who called themselves the Anti-Lynching Crusaders, as well as many investigative journalist and educators, wrote newspaper articles exposing the torturous murders. They unwrapped and exposed this common vigilante act that was committed frequently in the South.

To understand the impact that the torturous song made, go to the internet and listen to her mournful cries that catapulted a revolt against the merciless acts. If you have a heart, it is impossible to listen to the melody and lyrics without feeling deep compassion for the injustice and corporate sins of our nation. After all, if we are not part of the solution, we are part of the problem.

Warning: It's a tearjerker that terrorizes sensitive hearts. Put the kids to bed until they are old enough to hear and learn from this historical horror story that helped change our rude history.

Moving from horrifying to sublime, I wanted to see the Broadway musical *Jelly's Last Jam* in New York City. It is about the life and music of Jelly Roll Morton, who published one of the first jazz compositions in 1902 and is considered the founding father of jazz as a musical form. Acting greats such as Ben Vereen, Gregory Hines, and Phylicia Rashad were all going to be on one stage, together, telling the fascinating life story of Jelly Roll Morton!

Since we made a habit to run around the Big Apple every five years or so just to feast our ears and eyes, Spurgeon took me to see the play on my birthday that year.

We stayed in a tiny room in the center of Manhattan that we found, of course, through our *New York on $100 a Day* book. Incredibly, the hotel offered free parking for the duration of our stay! (Spurgeon told the attendant to bury it for the entire week. We enjoyed walking and public transport.) That August 14th birthday in the Big Apple was sultry and steamy hot. Sweating as we stood in the "Hot Ticks" line to buy half price tickets for plays that were not sold out that day, we salivated when the Italian Ice vender came near enough to hail. He made money hand-over-fist with the patient line of theater buffs. The lemon ice we chose, mixed with drips from a sweaty upper lip, tasted heaven sent. We continued to wait in line and reached out our hands to receive any restaurant coupons that were offered to us. French cuisine was our exquisite choice that day, two for the price of one! Fun, fun, fun!

After the delightful five-course French dinner, we sauntered toward the *Jelly's Last Jam* theater. Seating ourselves, we began reading our program flyer. Immediately, we were impressed by the humility expressed by Ben Vereen in the credits of the program. He had experienced a serious car accident and, in place of a lengthy list of his accomplishments, these words were written under his name, "From now on my every breath is for the Lord." He won our hearts!

"God gives us all things that we might enjoy" (1 Timothy 6:17, paraphrased).

CHAPTER 11

Emotional Intelligence Trumps

BACK IN THE '50S and '60s, all Minnesota students took an I.Q. test. At the time, the test measured one's intellect in regard to base knowledge, problem solving, and some creative thinking. In those days, the test was not only culturally biased, but it failed to measure vital wellness issues, such as socio/emotional intelligence, as they presently do. I have often wished that Spurgeon had access to the current I.Q. test, as he is an emotional savant. Allow me to demonstrate with a few stories.

Spurgeon had a most unique and highly effective way of nailing what he had to say. For example, a good man who wants to assure his wife of his allegiance might say something like, "I only have eyes for you." This would bring a smile to his wife's heart.

Spurgeon found a unique way of bringing a smile to my heart one day as we traveled in a small caravan from the Midwest to Raleigh, South Carolina, for a family gathering to honor "favorite niece," Fannie, in her retirement. Brother William called Spurgie on the cell phone and said we should all go straight to the seafood restaurant instead of the house, because everyone was hungry. Spurgie told me the plan, and I retorted, "Oh, oh, Rosie's not going to like that. She has a seafood allergy."

Pausing slightly, shrugging his shoulders, he dryly responded, "I don't sleep with Rosie."

Taking me by surprise, I looked at his serious face and said, "Well, yah, I know that!"

Momentarily, I took another peek at him to see if there was more to the message. His straight face told me he was finished.

"So," I said, not willing to pass this one up, "that means you don't care about another woman's opinion, because you don't sleep with her?"

"Right." He was quietly adamant.

Amused and pleased, I let that one fly.

But I have thought about the profundity of its placement and execution many times since. If ever a man wanted his wife to get a clear-cut message that he truly cares about her feelings, and hers alone, this is an effective line. I give it to all you loving husbands out there. But, forewarned is forearmed. One must be a husband of huge integrity in order to execute that line effectively!

Back at the farm in Michigan, we had a living room that was 28'x 28' and we used it like a ballroom. The couches faced each other in the middle of the room, and sparse furniture lined the edges. However, we had ample space to dance around the furniture and have evening soirees. We would spin old jazz vinyls and dance and romance.

We burned wood and had a wonderful fireplace for warmth but needed some serious underwear for outdoor Michigan life. In Chicago, neither of us owned long underwear, as most of our activities were indoors in the winter.

Not so in Southwestern Michigan. We now hauled wood in daily, skated and slid onto the frozen pond, hunted, and four-wheeled all throughout the cold weather. So, I bought a navy blue, two-piece, long-underwear set for Spurgeon and a red, two-piece set for me. This particular night we both donned our new, waffled outfits and spun vinyl, dancing to Nat King Cole, Louie Armstrong, and the Staple Singers.

After a few rounds, Spurgeon delighted me by a dip in our boogie! As he dipped me, his resonant voice, drenched with a fake French accent, purred in my ear, "My Dear, you look divine in your lovely red gown from Paris!"

First, I giggled. Giggles turned to peals of laughter. We two jubilant jointly and gently fell to the floor, still entwined. We lay on the hardwood and spoke more fake French, sparkling eyes enraptured. He was such a fun trip! A more tender love could not be found.

He was all about romance in our friends' lives too. After about a year of dating, our good buddies, Kim and Mary, decided they were going to elope to Niagara Falls. We gamed one night at their house, when they casually told us of their penciled-in plans. It was our normal time to leave, at 1:00 a.m.

Readying for bed that night, Spurgeon asked me if I'd ever been to Niagara Falls. I said I had been there briefly on my way to New York many years ago. He excitedly shared that he'd never been and would really like to go. He said he was going to call Mary and Kim and tell them that we were going to Niagara also. He wanted to marry our friends off and spend a couple of days there ourselves, just exploring. He was totally stoked about this!

"Spurgeon, did you ever think that maybe they would like to go by themselves, and we would be an intrusion?"

"Oh, no. Not at all! I know they would love to have us stand up for them!"

"Well at least wait until morning to call. It's late!"

Spurgeon was at Mary and Kim's door when they awoke the next day! He excitedly shared that we were going to go ahead, get a place with a view, and take them to a nice pre-wedding dinner on their arrival. Then, we could stand up for them, give them the rings, and bid them a wonderful honeymoon.

They loved the plan!

Mary later told me that they were so tickled with Spurgeon's enthusiasm and that his suggestions helped them solidify their plans.

The wedding was in a beautiful chapel with white flowing chiffon curtains and white pillars. A fabulously friendly, Christian minister married them in our presence.

None of us can imagine it being any different than the way it went.

Though Mary and Kim were part of our daily lives in Michigan, Spurgeon referred to, throughout the years, one of his enduring friendships in his young adult life. He had sadly lost track of Harold.

Harold (once I finally met him) resembled a tall, verbose, German American Jew with a hint of a Yiddish accent. They had met each other when both of them were in their mid-twenties, while taking several body shop classes together in Chicago. They became fast friends, studied together, and ran together socially.

Down the line in years, as they raised their respective families, they lost track of each other. Spurgie would mention Harold every now and then, wondering what his life was about.

One of these contemplative days, when my guy bemoaned not having contact with his old buddy, a light turned on in my attic, and I went to the internet to search on the site called "Switchboard." It is a computer form of the old-fashioned telephone book. Checking in the rough area where he lived thirty years prior, I found Harold's name and number and handed it to Spurgeon.

Delighted, he immediately made the call and reached his old study buddy. The conversation was long, loud, and riotous! After catching up on decades of personal information, they agreed that Harold and wife, Alice, would drive out to Michigan to visit.

I was tickled over their renewed relationship. They man-hugged, slapped backs, drew apart to look at each other, and pulled in to embrace again! The "Do you remember when . . . " stories bounced off the walls.

As they expressed their joy in seeing one another again, Harold slung his arm around Spurgie once more and, smiling broadly, told me: "This man is my true brother. He might have a different mother, but he is my brother!"

He was stating the obvious.

These fine visits were repeated for a couple years, until Alice fell ill and died. One night, about a year after Alice passed, a call came from Harold's son, who was caring for his fast-ailing father. "Dad wants to talk with you, Spurgeon."

The weakened voice of this darling, gentle giant spoke. "Brother, I had to call and tell you that I love you one more time before I die. I'll be waiting for you on the other side."

This wonderful, warm, color-blind friend passed away later that evening. It remains one of the sweetest friendships I've ever witnessed.

As good as he was at making long-term friends, Spurgeon also made quick friendships. That was demonstrated well when we rode our mountain bikes in a public park not too far from home and ran into trouble with a local. I was monumentally grateful for Spurgeon's acute sense of diplomacy that had been exhibited on numerous occasions and marveled as he handled this very angry individual.

While cruising the forest with our mountain bikes, we unwittingly crossed unto private property. A size-large farmer dressed in bib overalls with a heavy steel shovel in one hand appeared directly in the path and startled us with a heavy, irate, "This is private property, and you have no right to be here!"

With his face hot and red with anger, he put fear in me.

Spurgie's response was immediate and humble. "Well, sir, I certainly understand you being upset. No one wants trespassers. Worse yet, people who don't even know they are trespassing. Maybe we could ask the campground to put up some kind of barrier or signs, so that hikers and bikers will know the boundaries and not intrude on your property. Please accept our apology Mr. . . . ?"

And as he spoke these words, dripping with sincerity, he extended his hand to the distressed stranger. The large man pondered Spurgeon's words, stared at the outstretched hand, and contemplated a response.

Slowly, he lowered his hand from the shovel, leaned it against a tree, and met my hero's hand. "Kruger is the name."

My snake-charmer husband continued in light conversation. Before we left, Mr. Kruger suggested, "Maybe we'll see each other around town!"

It wasn't magic. It was more like deep wisdom.

Spurgeon's sage behavior extended to child discipline also. The following story was only humorous to us as parents at the time. Now, our children are grown, and we all laugh about it.

We all make mistakes, some more consistently than others. We all deserve a second chance, in most instances. So, Spurgeon and I instituted the strike system in our home. One strike, shame on you. Two strikes, shame on us if we continue to take abuse. Three strikes and there will be real consequences, in accordance with the wrong done.

Two of our kids, his and ours, at distinctly different times, insisted on expressing their anger by culminating a conversation with us by slamming the door while retreating to their bedrooms. Unwilling to allow this disrespect, when next in their presence, Spurgeon gently stated there will be no door slamming in our home, and they'd just received a strike one.

In the case of door slamming, strike three resulted in the removal of the door of their bedroom. The door was then parked in a corner of the garage. It was restored to its rightful position when the appropriate attitude was displayed, along with an apology. We never had to repeat the consequence on any one child.

I got a real kick out of one of his parenting statements, dropping it on other people when they rashly stated what their kids would and would not do. He would grin, light up those eyes and state, "I'll tell you *exactly* what my kids will and will not do . . . when they are in front of my face." Funny how that was generally followed by chuckles and a change in subject matter.

Sometimes this guy of mine had the most ingenious cures for people's social discomforts. We had graduated to a camper after the tent was no longer practical and drove to visit my cousin in Colorado. She had two gorgeous daughters in their late teens. We planned to stay two weeks, breaking the cardinal rule of "fish and company are only good for three days." Though Spurgie initially objected to the lengthy stay, we found that visiting in a camper takes a big burden off the host.

Each night, after work, school, or a full day of touring Denver's attractions, we met in the house or the camper to play games, a big part of our family fun. As families go, the teens, Sommer and Ashley, were different as night and day. Ash took speedily to communicating with both Spurgeon and me. Som, a reserved, shy girl, was cautious and watchful. Spurgie and I wondered how we might help her with social reticence but had no ready solutions. So, we prayed about it.

About three or four nights into the visit, Som sat next to Spurgeon during a tempestuous game of Hand and Foot. Shortly into the game, Som accidentally bumped Spurgie's elbow. Quick as a wink, Spurgeon looked sternly at the teen and admonished her with, "You don't know me well enough to touch me!"

The whole table of players froze instantly. Shock registered on every face but the speaker's. His was blank. I had never heard a harsh word come from the man's mouth, ever. We were all stunned. In the seconds that the shock wore off, Spurgeon's eyes then began to twinkle as he peered at Som. Suddenly, he busted into mirthful laughter, as did we all.

The next day, Som had off both school and work. She arranged to go with us on our trip to Boulder. She became our shadow after that, and we made a fun trio. We enjoyed our teases and barbs, as we journeyed, finding fun and knowledge.

Spurgeon shared his humor on an international level also. We were privileged to form a couple of labor mission teams, each consisting of sixteen workers. We worked with Paul and Marty in Peru, South America. They are lifers with Union Biblical, or Scripture Union, and the couple I worked with fifteen years earlier when I lived in Peru. Life had come full circle and now my adventurous man and I were building a short-term mission team.

Our teams, along with many other teams from around the United States and world, helped build orphanages for the street boys in Peru, of which there were many.

Spurgeon, a hardworking, knowledgeable man in the area of building trade, got along famously with the Peruvian plumber, Raul. Spurgie spoke in pidgin Spanish while Raul spoke in pidgin English. They plumbed and laughed, looking like two schoolboys enjoying the playground.

Raul the plumber and his buddy, Spurgeon

At one point, both plumbers were kneeling on the jungle floor, while chickens clucked around them catching insects. Spurgeon cocked his head to listen, stopped working, and put his index finger to his lips. Alerted, Raul listened intently. Spurgeon whispered, "Whoa, that's strange."

"*Que?*" ["What?"] Raul whispered back.

"Well, here I am in Peru and you're *hablando español* [speaking Spanish], which I'm trying hard to learn. But your Peruvian *pollos* [chickens] speak English, exactly like mine in Michigan!"

Raul leaned into his friend as they chuckled together.

The strongest trait making Spurgeon outstandingly compassionate was his intrigue with people and his superior listening skills. Megan, a youth in our church, expressed this best. "I could bare my soul to him, make myself vulnerable, and trust him not to crush me." He was that way with everyone he met.

My cousin, Julie, who I mentioned before, along with her husband, Kelly, teach therapeutic art to at-risk high schoolers. Relational issues sometimes arise. She tells her students, citing Spurgeon and me: "The most successful relationships are steeped in good manners. My favorite cousin and her husband never forget to be polite with each other. They say please, thank you, could you, will you, may I, in each conversation, generally accompanied by a pet name. Politeness breeds positive communication."

On semi-regular intervals in our marriage, Spurgeon coaxed me into sitting on the couch with no music, sound, or outside interference. Just talk. Since that practice was unfamiliar to me, it took me by surprise. He would pick a weekend evening and say, "Come sit on the couch with me, put your beautiful legs in my lap, and let me stare into those stunning blue eyes."

Now, how could any wife refuse that invitation? We would sit and talk about everything and nothing until we were talked out, laughed out, and ready for bed. We talked of gratitude for the way the God had so obviously blessed us. We gave thanks for our progressive life in Him, growth in faith, and the joy of sharing our lives together. We thanked God for giving us a little bit of heaven on earth through our marriage. We talked about past, present and future. We shared deep emotions, things that we'd never told other people. These were always precious, precious times.

Emotional intelligence runs in Spurgeon's family. It skips some family members but is prominent in the character of several others, one being our youngest granddaughter, Tyler.

One visiting summer, when TyTy was about seven, she entered my art studio, came over, leaned up against me, and peered at my work. While perusing, she queried, "Deb, why did you do it that way?"

"Well, I just didn't want to do it like everybody else," I answered, happy she was observant enough to notice.

Immediately stepping to one side with wide open eyes, then hands on the hips, she announced, "Oh, Deb, not to worry. No one would ever mistake you for normal!"

Now that was an astute observation for a seven-year-old!

One day Spurgeon and I read an article that encouraged couples to, on quiet, contemplative nights, ask crucial questions about life. There were several deep queries, so it was sometimes a one-question night, but it did tend to bring out innate or pent-up feelings.

Some of the questions we've asked over the years are:

> What is your earliest recollection of your childhood?
> What were some of your strongest childhood memories?
> What do you consider your greatest successes?
> To what do you attribute those successes?
> If you could pick anyone throughout history up to now, who would you pick as your hero? Why?
> What is your favorite scripture? Under what circumstances did you adopt it as such?
> What do you believe your spiritual gifts to be?
> How did you discover them? Are you utilizing them?
> What are the top three happiest times of your life?
> What was the most trying time of your life? Do you like the way you handled it?
> What was the most fascinating time in your life?
> What experience made your grow up fast?
> Tell me of a favorite time with each of your children. And your grandchildren.
> Do you have a bucket list? What is on it?
> What experience would you like to have lived without?
> What is the best advice that you've ever been given? How did it work in your favor?
> Do you have a bucket list? What is on it?
> Do you like the way we handle our affairs? Are you happy?
> How can we improve ourselves as a couple?
> What is the most pressing prayer on your heart?

There are any number of conversational questions you might ask your spouse. And, though many couples may think this a hokey exercise, it produces fascinating conversations. The predominant benefit of these exchanges is that they help each spouse learn how to best encourage his or her mate according to that person's strengths and weaknesses, likes and dislikes. It taught us to help each other be the best we could be.

With open hearts used consistently, this sharing can make for a highly productive relationship, and evening.

No time to just sit? Give up a television night. It's an excellent enhancement to more intimate lives.

Another reason the above conversations are so effective for our well-being is because no one takes the time to ask such pertinent questions of each other. Bad information shared is still a burden off the heart of the teller. Good information shared lends joy to the listener and teller. Intimacy grows exponentially.

So, sharing our intimate lives with the right person is healthy and cathartic. Try it. You'll like it. And sometimes the honesty will challenge you.

One night, as we sat on the loveseat facing each other, a weighty statement came from my lover's lips. "Do you realize that you have been ignoring me for your art?"

Stunned, the statement was an anvil on my shoulders. In total sincerity, I responded, "No, Darling, I had no idea."

"Ever since you joined the 'Art Girlz' (my longstanding art club of a dozen or so multi-media area artists), you have embedded yourself in art, and you have neglected time with me."

Though it was not his intention, I was ashamed to my core. I have always wanted to be a Biblical wife, one who devotes her time to her husband and family. That I had carelessly disregarded my priorities flabbergasted me. I had no idea I'd made my most precious love lonely. He had approached this delicate subject with gentility, wisdom, and self-control.

We finished out the discussion, as I thanked him for being so transparent. I do not know of many men who would approach the subject of discomfort so honestly and tactfully. It was another reason why people responded to him so positively.

Well, I immediately cut back on my playing hours in my art studio and focused on being with Spurgie, doing fun or laborious tasks, as working farms require. If he was involved in a task, I knew nothing about, he still enjoyed my being in his presence, sitting, and observing and chatting as he worked. I was extremely grateful to Spurgeon for being honest with me. That took bravery, love, and humility.

On another of these heartwarming loveseat occasions, my tone went flat as sadness overcame me. Noting the change in my demeanor, Spurgie asked, "Amor, what's wrong? You look far away and sad."

I was reticent to share this particularly profound hurt, even with him,

Afraid he might think it silly or immature on my part, I'd kept this feeling inside. He asked me to share, if I could, stressing that if I couldn't tell him, then who could I tell? Knowing that he was right and that telling might diminish the power of the pain, I shared.

Hesitantly, I began. "All my life I mourned the parents that I never knew." (You will remember from Chapter Two that my mom and dad were dead, one year apart, by the time I was four years old.) "I feel sad that they birthed me and my brothers but didn't get to raise us. And I miss them. I realize that probably sounds totally lame coming from a grown woman, but it has been a weighty issue for me all my life."

Even as the words slipped from my lips, tears formed in my lower lids.

My insides cringed, wondering what he would think. I hardly dared look up at him.

He tenderly responded, "Oh, *Amor*. I see you. I hear you. That is not a silly thought. I understand that perfectly. Come here and let me hold you."

That was the last time I mourned my parents' death! The power of death was removed by Love. Again. I was more grateful for and more impressed with this man who defied so many odds and made my life felicitous.

CHAPTER 12

It Can't Be Just All Roses

AT THIS POINT IN the script, the reader may think, "Well, no one person and no couple is perfect. There had to be some bad days, arguments, dissidence, or verbal bantering. There just had to be."

Well, yah!

It was a quiet evening only months into our perfect marriage when Spurgeon, for no apparent reason, opened a conversation with: "You do realize that I will disappoint you sometime. I won't mean to. And you will disappoint me sometime, not wanting to. It will happen because we are human. And being human and being hurt are synonymous with each other."

That set a stage for a softer landing once we fell.

The everyday garden variety of discord seldom surfaced. We enjoyed the heck out of each other and were thrilled to spend life together. With seventeen years difference in our ages, we knew from the start we had to take advantage of the time we were given. We felt God had favored us by putting us together, so we gleefully made the best of it.

Nonetheless, we actually had four memorable spats and one shocking readjustment.

The first biggie happened about six months into our blissful marriage. It was a complete control issue on my part, accompanied by a hefty dose of lack of trust. I now relate my behavior to residual effects of my former marriage. It was sufficiently embarrassing, as to guarantee that I won't repeat that behavior. I was all wet, recognized it immediately, asked forgiveness and received it. Thank God.

We taught each other a three-step, good apology:

1). I was wrong.

2). I am sorry.

3). Please forgive me.

I don't remember where we learned this, but we implemented this excellent tool of understanding anytime needed.

But truth be told, this is my philosophy: "We all have a right to be stupid now and then. We just can't abuse the privilege!" This comes in handy, if one falls into the self-deprecating mode. I learned that from Jen, one of our heart girls we've known since she wore diapers and who went on the first mission trip to Peru.

Deb, Jen, our heart-girl, and Spurgeon in Peru

The next big argument, one the family likes to laugh about, concerns Spurgie's stated restriction on my having a dog. Our first dog at the farm lived fifteen years. Roxie was an Australian shepherd/lab mix and was the best farm dog ever. She protected our domestic rabbits and chickens while she ate whole nests of wild hares! She picked up the miscellaneous eggs the chickens failed to lay in their nests and placed them on our doormat. They lay there until we got up and found them. She enjoyed the twenty acres and didn't leave the farm. She killed the woodchucks that lived under our sheds. She jumped in the pond on hot summer days and enjoyed a good swim. She loved to be near us.

When she passed, I found myself yearning for another second-best friend. It seemed like a part of me was missing without a canine. So, when I went to run errands, unbeknownst to hubby, I often stopped at the Cass County Animal Shelter. I wanted to see if there were any dogs that might be crazy about me and vice versa. After a half-dozen visits, I found what I thought to be another Australian Shepherd mix and brought the seven-month-old shepherd/lab home. She was exactly what I wanted. Hubby, however, was not happy. He grumbled, repeatedly and often, and sternly stated, "I thought we said no more dogs."

My only comeback, head bowed, was a sheepish, "Yah, that's what *you said*. But, I never agreed to that."

No visible response.

The next day we were sitting on the grand 12' x 36' deck that Spurgeon built me for my birthday. It was the second day for the new puppy. We were having our morning coffee and devotions when dear, little Shadow whined at the bottom of the four-step stairs. She had evidently never experienced steps before and didn't know how to navigate them. I heard her but was reticent to let her up because of Spurgeon's feelings.

"Your dog is crying. She wants up," stated my husband.

"Yah, I know. . . . Her name is Shadow. I thought she would be a reminder of your disapproval, so I left her there . . . crying." The last word of that sentence was thrown in for effect.

Without a word, Spurgeon got up from the lounge chair, retrieved the pup from the lawn, and put her on my lap. "I've always heard that women and cats will do as they please. Men and dogs must get use to the idea."

I felt a bit chagrinned at that statement, but, head still bowed in humility, I silently let it pass.

He ended up loving the dog, which made him stop mentioning that I got her against his will. But it was my bad, sort of.

Little Shadow, all grown up

Now here is one on Spurgeon. If you think that he is sounding pretty flawless by now, you are perceptive. But alas, all good behavior comes to an end! At least I have one example of his demeanor that is boldly unbecoming! I must share the details with you.

We have a couple of friends and family who could well be defined as hoarders. So, Spurgie and I had serious discussions on how full (or empty) we want our space. Our home is modestly furnished and decorated artistically. I have a tendency to collect beautiful things, because I was brought up a third-generation rummage saler. Plus, my mixed-media art requires lots of stuff.

But I am blessed with a healthy case of claustrophobia. I cannot and will not be closed in. This helps me maintain a healthy balance of material things without overload.

When we moved from the farm to the lake just around the corner, we had to size down drastically. We were ready, taxing as it was, to go from a rambling ranch on twenty acres with a double garage and multiple outbuildings to a little cottage on three quarters of an acre.

We did it. And we were not crowded.

We agreed we would not bring anything into the house that was not consumable. If we did adopt an item, we got rid of something else. We were both perfect with that verbal contract for six whole years.

Then came the fateful day at the Artisan Shoppe, when I dropped off some of my art for sale. I eyed a fellow artist's welded, metal portrayal of a snake. It was amazingly creative. The slinky part of the body was made of a bicycle chain with flattened steal head, forked tongue and ball bearing rattler tail sticking straight up. I couldn't resist it. After all, I could find something to get rid of. And, given the subject matter, it could be an indoor or outdoor piece of art. Oh, yah, I could justify this snake.

Excitedly, I stepped into the living room to show Spurgie the captivating critter. It was such a masculine-looking little thing, I was certain this man of taste and distinction would appreciate it.

He glanced at my rattler and quipped sneeringly, "You're going to stuff this house as full as ----'s!"

Ohhhh. I knew he didn't go there! I just knew he wouldn't do that!

But he did! And I was livid! I was so hot I couldn't speak, because I was sure to say something ugly and mean, just to hurt him. So, I turned around and, with *great* maturity, stomped down to my art room in the basement. Far away from him, I steamed.

I steamed silently until I could pray. I prayed with fervor for grace and peace and self-control. I did breathing exercises with long exhales. I did art for about two hours, until I felt confident I'd received the gifts for which I'd asked. Then I went upstairs to calmly approach my husband and tell him that he owed me an apology.

Standing before him and looking straight into his eyes with as much love as possible, I jump-started the message. "You owe me. . . "

"Yes! I know! I do! I'm sorry. I'm *so* sorry," he interrupted, reached his hand up as a sign of peace and grabbed mine.

"Okay."

It was over.

Now we both think the snake is unique.

And would you believe I can't remember what the other argument was about? Truly! The remembrance of high emotional volatility is strong, but not the subject matter. There is a hefty recollection of me being agitated about whatever the problem was.

It was a dark summer night, and I walked around the one-acre pond in the pitch black to let off steam. Returning to the house, I stopped where our favorite vintage glider stood.

Snake art by Jeff Zimmerman

After a few minutes of my sitting and rocking, Spurgeon came out of the house and sat and rocked with me in silence. We inched our hands into a clasp and slowly leaned all over each other without a word.

Whatever the problem was, the glider worked it out.

Cuz Jules and Spurgeon on the glider that resolves all

The skeptics among you who read this will say, "Nah. There had to be more harsh times than that. Nobody skates by for thirty-seven years without wading into much deeper water."

And though I am not a skeptic in the least, I would understand that.

One enjoyable tradition in churches I've attended all over the nation is personal testimony time. Our culture makes light of "sinner to saint" stories, even when the change of the individual is real and lasting. I think it's because since the early 1950s, our nation has been defined as a "post Christian nation." The United States of America has not been a Christian country for decades now. It shows in our character.

But one day in a Sunday morning service, a matriarch of the church gave her life testimony. I had never heard anything like it before. "Oh, I had godly parents and a beautiful husband who gave me wonderful children, who were joyful to raise, and I just can't say anything but 'Thank you, God.'"

On the way home from church that day, I attacked the testimony. "Can you believe what she said? Never a problem! Perfect parents, perfect husband, perfect kids, perfect life! That is ridiculous! Why would she say that? No one grows up, gets old and is blissful the whole time. That is not real."

Spurgie, while driving, gave me a side glance with a slight scowl as he stated, "Wow, Deb. That sounds jaded on your part. Some people do have really good lives, escaping hardships, somehow. Don't be mad at her because she had an uneventful, unscathed time on earth. It's not like you to be jealous."

Now, my husband, who has known hard times in his life, from child labor and near starvation, to bias and meanness, came out and declared life can exist pain free?

I did not fall for his line. But, since then, I worked with a woman in our community whom I know to be a realist. She said she knows people who claimed the same existence.

Nevertheless, our marriage was the closest I ever came to heaven on earth, but it followed an ugly, early life on both our parts. So, I am hard pressed to not believe "in this world you will have trouble" (John 16:33, NIV).

We tried warding off harshness between us before it began. Both of us are a peaceful sort, and both of us were nuts about each other. We were supplied with wonderful connectedness, which allowed us to avert many issues by excellent communication. We did not take each other for granted and consistently used polite verbiage. We said please and thank you because "love is not rude." We agreed to not make assumptions. No letting the sun go down on wrath. We learned early in our relationship that the more time we spent together, the happier we were. And being retired young promoted that desire. We learned to relish constructive criticism. We did daily devotions together, so that we would "grow more and more in love so that we might determine what is best" (Philippians 1: 9–10). We delighted in our togetherness.

And we checked on each other when venturing on an improvement plan.

I remember after a social event in our home, Spurgeon gently took me aside and told me I might consider cutting down on my exaggerations. He cited a specific example from the evening that made my listener raise an eyebrow. Embarrassed to recognize the truth, I took a good look at my personality and considered it might be one of those sins that "easily beset me" (Hebrews 12:1, paraphrased). After all, I am an artist and storyteller. I believe it common knowledge that our weaknesses often lie very close to our strengths.

Taking that observation/criticism earnestly, I set about disciplining myself for the change. A year down the line, I asked Spurgeon how I was doing. Beaming, he declared the improvement was more than substantial.

That was only one of our approaches to positive change. We were proactive in preventive techniques in order to enhance our daily communications. Spurgeon had a fluidity of speech and behavior that was inoffensive. I, on the other hand, am more impulsive and have occasionally verbalized things that unwittingly hurt or offended people. Though I am not shy to say I am sorry, it is frequently like putting a bandage on a wound.

We discussed these offenses in prayer and ended up with the best solution we could think of. Our daily prayer became: "Let the words of my mouth, and the meditation of my heart, be acceptable in thy sight, O LORD, my strength, and my redeemer" (Psalms 19:14, KJV).

God is so much more even-tempered and aware of the heart's intentions than we humans. If we don't offend Him by our thoughts, then we figure we should be fairly safe with earthlings. Mostly.

CHAPTER 13

Party Place

DOWN ON THE TWENTY-acre farm with its pond, forest, and beauty, we hosted a number of memorable parties, especially Spurgeon's seventieth birthday.

He had just overcome, by God's great touch, a hefty case of prostate cancer. It was a landmark healing. Our seven-year-old Bible study group collaborated with us.

Two surgeons opinionated that Spurgeon should have the problem cut out. Because of the advanced disease of the prostate, incontinence as well as impotence would likely follow the surgery. We honestly felt God would not want that for Spurgeon, because he was so "young" and vitally active. God assured us He had a great deal more for Spurgie to do in his life. Therefore, we accepted the council of a third medical advisor, the American Cancer Institute, and went on a program of organic juicing, fasting, and praying.

We purchased the best juicer on the market, one that spun at a slower revolution than its competitors. High speeds heat the mash and juice, destroying vital, healing nutrients. Organic carrots, apples, and cabbage were our main juice ingredients. If we were still hungry and had to satisfy that chewing desire, we were to eat an organic lettuce salad with a dash of apple-cider vinegar and a few organic peanuts. We diligently devoted ourselves to this diet for two months, praying in God's will.

When that timeframe was up, Spurgeon returned to have a biopsy, one more time. The tumor had completely dissolved. We were unendingly grateful and elated over this favor from God.

After he received that clean bill of health, I started planning, in secret, his birthday party. While Spurgeon resumed the farm chores, I made food for the day in duplicate and put one recipe in the freezer to start building up dishes. I mobilized friends, assigning my power people to direct groups and pay the pulled-pork cook and port-a-potty deliveries while Spurgeon and I were out. Mary and Kim (whom we married off in Niagara), as part of the plot, asked us out for a leisurely breakfast the morning of the party, so the family could set up the farm. They brought in and set up a port-o-potty in an obvious place. The fresh pulled-pork guy came in with his cooker and set up near the food tables. An old kindergarten sand table with galvanized aluminum was filled with ice for all the salads and cold foods. Family and friends coming from a short distance were asked to bring dishes.

Family from afar brought a barrel of live crawdads up from Mississippi! And the most outrageous Black Forest Cherry cake came from the much-loved Jarosch Bakery in Chicago! Everyone wanted to do something special for this fine man.

For entertainment, I hired a four-piece jazz band with two guitars, an alto saxophone, and percussion. We'd heard them play at a friend's wedding reception and we really liked their music. I put them under one of the giant tents. The second tent was for food.

By the time the four of us arrived from breakfast, party balloons decorated the mailbox, and our son, on the four-wheeler, was directing traffic. One hundred and thirty-seven people, from three countries and seven states, waited to greet the birthday guy. Spurgeon's mind was blown! A friend followed him around with a video recorder, and utter shock registered on his face for the first hour of the film.

I would like to take credit for keeping the party a secret, but it was the internet that really helped me. Spurgie resorts to computers only out of necessity, and I steered him away during the months of planning.

At the conclusion of this marvelous day, I walked over to talk with the band as they packed up their equipment. We had invited them to partake in the food, when they took a break, and they hadn't hesitated. The leader of the band told me: "I have eaten my way from Chicago to Detroit, and I have never had a feedbag like you have here today!" I believe that!

It was an immense pleasure for me to see darling Spurgeon so happy. He spoke of that day many times for years.

The party house and pond

Later, down the line, I planned a pajama party and art weekend at our home with a group of my besties for my sixtieth birthday. Spurgeon agreed to be my personal gopher for the weekend.

It was to begin on a Saturday morning with a late, gourmet waffle breakfast. Two art projects were scheduled for the afternoon, with spaces for walking around the pond, finding photo ops, taking a dip, fishing in the pond, or sipping homemade lemonade on the deck.

I invited a few artists who come from Berrien Springs, Michigan, home of Andrews University, a Seventh Day Adventist facility. Most Adventists are vegetarian. Each month when The Art Girlz met, we cooked and had a smorgasbord via potluck. So, I was well acquainted with their culinary delights.

Preparing many dishes ahead was assurance meals would be nutritious and delicious. Plus, we had the added benefit that my birthday is in August, and Spurgeon's gourmet garden was full-fledged during that month. We partied organically!

We celebrated all day. In the evening we crowned the queen who won the best-skit contest. Skinny dipping in the lake after midnight was optional. . . . I won't rat on my friends, though.

A campout for the weekend with friends from church became yet another enormous party at the farm. A real kicker of a weekend! From the embryonic stage, we knew the idea would be pregnant. A planning committee was formed. Spurgie and I would do setup, and everyone would clean up, Shelly planned the entertainment, Miriam organized the food, another arranged group devotions.

Campfire wood was supplied for a perpetual fire. Each of the six campers brought their own extension cords. We staged them around the ample yard, so as not to overload any one circuit. A half dozen tents popped up all round the pond. Croquet and volleyball games sprung up here and there between planned events. For three days, our church family camped, cooked, laughed, swam, fished, played games, sang, and just hung out.

One of the teen boys slept on our hard metal glider for two nights. When I asked if we could find a more comfortable spot for him to sleep, he protested, "Oh, no, I have the best spot right here! I'm right in front of the dock. The girls keep going there to dangle their feet, and then I talk with them!"

There was a method to his madness.

One of the adorable teen girls, Brittany, asked me, "Can I swim in the pond?"

"Well, we have a lot of snapping turtles, so we don't swim during the summer. But it is September, and they have gone into hibernation."

"Do you sometimes swim in it this time of year?"

"No, this has a mucky bottom. We have Kelsey Lake with a sandy beach at the end of our property, so we just go there," I answered, throwing a hint.

"You mean this is a *virgin pond*?" Brittany's face lit up with expectation.

"As far as I know it is."

And that is all it took! She ran for the family camper, changed to her swimsuit and dashed unto the dock, diving in headfirst.

That, of course, started a chain reaction and all the guys, young and old, had to cannon-ball each other as they jumped in! The virgin pond was no more.

Later on that Saturday afternoon, the main event was scheduled. Heads of households began setting up lawn chairs in a semicircle in front of the overhanging deck. In the side yard one of the girls set up a mock baseball diamond, spacing heavy rubber mats for bases.

Entering the house to gather personal equipment for my husband to use, our middle daughter, Linda, approached me with a puzzled face: "Deb, what in the world is going on here!? All the women are running around laughing and whispering with big bags in their hands. What's happening!?"

"We have a drag race planned for the husbands. We want the guys to know what it is like to be a woman and to have to perform certain tasks in clothes that are not suitable. So, each wife has made up a bag of clothes that will fit her husband that includes a dress, hat, purse (with specified contents), and high heels"

"Oh, my daddy is *not* going to put on any dress!" declared Linda.

"Well, he's not worn a dress in seventy-two years, so I suspect you're right, but I'm going to ask him anyway!"

Momentarily, Shelly blew the whistle. She announced over the loudspeaker the main event was ready to roll, so would all husbands come and sit down in the semicircle.

Accomplishing that, the instructor began: "We wives have worked hard to amass many articles for this event. We want it to be special for you, so we even have a handsome trophy for the winner." She held up the winged trophy.

"This is a Drag Race. Its ultimate goal is that all of you husbands realize the challenges and/or discomfort of dressing up in female attire, as we do for you and the world on a daily basis. When I give you the signal, each of you, in a leisurely manner, may put on each article of clothing in the bag before you. You will then line up on the starting line. When the whistle blows you will run, as best you can in your dress and heels, to first base. There you will open your purses, take out your pantyhose or nylons and put them on. Be certain not to rip holes in the stockings as you slide them on your legs. Replace your high heels and run to second base." Nervous smiles appeared on the men's faces.

Twelve of the ugliest women I've ever seen

Shelly continued explaining the dress code. "Arriving at second base, you must go inside your purse, remove the mirror and eye shadow and place the shadow on both your lids. When you are satisfied, show the monitor. If she approves, she will give you the okay and you can run for third base." Nervous looks turn concerned.

"At third base, you will open the purse and take out the lipstick. Apply it carefully, so as to pass inspection. Then, fast as you can, run for home base!"

"So, ladies, you may deliver your bags of clothing to your husbands, and on the count of three, men, you may start getting dressed!"

I must say, all those manly men peered into their bags and got started. Not one of them said no! Not even the oldest guy there, my handsome Spurgeon, who had never worn a dress! We think it was because of the artful way Shelly, the creator and announcer of the activity, downplayed the actual contents of the bag.

Families could help their head of households get dressed if they wished. Back buttons and side zippers befuddled these guys, as did multiple spaghetti-strapped dresses. Teen girls were a total hoot as they fitted their dads into sleek evening apparel, tugging and guffawing at the procedure. Tom strangled his neck after sticking his head between double straps. He needed his daughters' help!

When the whistle blew, these men in foreign clothes did their best to win the trophy and its dubious bragging rights! The men who ran the race finished with some understanding of the (sometimes) daily struggles of dressing up female.

Personally, I thought the winner's lipstick was far too smeared to pass inspection!

Incidentally, none of the men that I know of ever adopted this new fashion habit. *Uffda.*

One clarification to the reader: Spurgeon and I are near teetotalers. We were a true party place, but our friends chose to honor our beliefs in that area. All this fun happened without one mind-altering substance. We have found that where the Spirit of God is, there is joy.

And at times, hilarity.

Sixty-seven people camped the weekend with us. Everyone left just a little more in love with their church family. We didn't swear each other to secrecy, but we did take plenty of photos, so there is no denying who ran the Drag Race. It may surprise the reader how many pillars of the community were present.

Not always in fiesta mode, in everyday life we partied with table games. Spurgeon and I had an ongoing competition at all times between the two of us to see who could win twenty games of "Hand and Foot" first. We played one game a day, if possible, for about twenty years.

We found playing games to be a healthy interchange, not just for family but also friends. Games teach competition, help the mind master math, memory or other mind skills, and produce peals of laughter. Plus, we found it's the most sophisticated way of legitimately teasing those around you. I could totally get over on Spurgie one night and razz him all the way to bed. Then, we played the next night and it happened in reverse! The wonderful family banter began.

All our friends and family learned to enjoy the popular game of "Hand and Foot" that has swept the nation. We found it to be the most popular game in campgrounds all over the U.S. Our youngest grandbaby, Tyler, learned her numbers and addition while playing "Hand and Foot!"

Get five decks of cards and go the back of this book, in the last chapter, and you will find the rules for this wonderful pastime!

CHAPTER 14

Healthy Busy

OVER THE YEARS, NUMEROUS friends said to us something to the tune of, "Gee, you two are so capable and giving, you must get tired of saying no to requests for your time and attention. I just hate to say no to anyone!"

That comment frequently led to a fascinating discussion because we were neither over-asked nor did we feel bad about saying no, in most circumstances.

We had long established we were seeking the plan that would give us the promised "hope and a future" of which God speaks (Jeremiah 29:11). We coupled that with, He gives us the "desire and the power to do what pleases Him" (Philippians 2:13, NLT). We learned that making God happy makes life fulfilling.

Furthermore, my lovely husband had a wonderful sense of balance between work and play. He worked hard, but often played equally hard. In the city, we worked and rehabbed a house, but we also took one month of vacation annually to retreat from the crowded urban life. On the farm we ran a good household, grew a huge garden with plenty to share, hunted, worked seventeen diverse flower beds throughout the big yard, raised chickens and rabbits for eggs and meat, camped, taught at the local junior college as an adjunct, accomplished our church ministries, acted as docents, and raised each of our three grandkids for a period of time. And we did whatever else our hands found to do.

One year to celebrate "Sister Day," my brother, Bob, sent me a hilarious email, perfect for people concerned about advancing the love of God each day. It was accompanied by a little drawing which said, "Sis, I wish you the kind of year where every day, the minute your feet hit the floor, Satan says, 'Oh, crap, she's up again!'"

We laughed and laughed and loved every iota of that philosophy: Make the evil one squirm!

Indeed, that is what we were working for!

We also liked to sit with homemade lemonade on the porch for an hour in the middle of a hot summer day. Table games came out most nights for fun family feuds. We slept in on cold or rainy days, enjoying a leisurely breakfast with robust, gourmet coffee. Walks around the pond were frequent, because we could always spot a deer, nesting birds, turtles laying eggs, or new flowers wafting their fragrance before us. The television was family time only and we all watched it or chose a book to read. (We didn't get into family computers until the late 1980s.) We entertained with frequency, playing rounds of pool or fishing out on the pond.

Learning that our son, Yermalay, was a natural night owl and enjoyed sleeping outdoors, we slept in the back yard now and then as a family. It would be on a weekend night preceded by a game or two of croquet. (People liked to play on our court because it was so expansive, about three-fourths the length of a football field.) Sleeping near the fire ring in our sleeping bags became a beautiful family habit.

Once, for a home-school assignment, Brittany, our fourth-grade granddaughter, was asked to describe her family and what they like to do. Accompanied by drawings, she wrote, "For entertainment, our family entertains other people at our home. You never know what you are going to eat, or who you are going to eat it with."

From the mouths of babes.

God blessed us with the most beautiful twenty-acre farm, way off the road, with a one-acre pond in the middle. The property was one-third home and garden, one-third forest, and one-third swamp.

Century-old climbing trees adorned the property perimeter. We thoroughly enjoyed our land.

When I attended Trinity College in Deerfield, Illinois, the Christian liberal arts institution encouraged its students to develop a lifelong habit: Pick one ministry in the church along with one volunteer job in the community and do them both well. Their philosophy was if each individual pursued those two involvements, the love of God would spread at a good pace.

I shared my alma mater's mindset with Spurgeon, when we'd started planning our lives together. He really liked the idea, so we ran with it our whole marriage. We found that working in the community brought validity to our faith.

Those civic duties engaged our lives for a good number of years. We helped found a youth center and coordinated the docent department of the Underground Railroad Society of Cass County. With both of these volunteer positions, we became embedded in this quiet community nestled in cornfields.

Sometimes it doesn't even have to be a true responsibility in order to be a ministry. For example, as both Spurgie and I enjoy baseball we faithfully attended church and local tribal league games. Over the years, we came to like, then love, one of the pitchers on the Pokagon Band team. John had an eye and an arm. His pitches were so hard to hit! We would marvel at his form and spoke with him each post game. Once in a while, when we saw him in the community, all three of us would embrace and chatter, mostly about baseball.

One year as we looked forward to leading a mission team to Peru, our seventeen-year-old friend, Rita, wanted to go. However, she needed to raise money for the trip. One of my art friends, Deane, suggested a community scholarship we could apply for on Rita's behalf. Not knowing anyone in this particular organization, we had no idea if it would come to pass. But we prayed we would get it.

All applicants were to attend a luncheon at a local restaurant, where the recipients would be announced. Our friend, Deane, picked us up, and we went to the luncheon together. We entered as two hundred people or more were eating their salads, so we didn't have a chance to socialize or see whom we might know. When people had eaten, Mark (later to become an honorable judge in our county) began calling names of the winners. Several recipients were named, and the monies and availability began winding down.

Then Mark held up one application and called out, "Here is an interesting application for a mission trip to South America, but I don't know the applicants. Does anyone know a S-p-u-r-g-e-o-n and Debbie Wiggins?"

Four hands, three of whose owners we were unaware, shot up in the crowded room!

"Yeah, give it to them," one vocalized.

"Yup, good people. Good cause," came the next raised hand.

"Absolutely," stated a voice that sounded familiar.

"They're valid," came the last hand.

Wow! They say a good name is worth gold. We didn't know a pitcher and catcher and two artists were going to defend our cause, but that was the end blessing. Rita got the scholarship.

And Rita deserved that monetary help! The whole trip cost $1,400, so she asked if she could bring us the rest of the money as she earned it. We agreed to be her bankers. One time she came with a weighty sack full of coins and change. Picking an exceedingly cold Michigan winter day to groom for greater success, she wore a two-sided sign on her torso that read "Will pump gas for free," on the front and on the back, "Peru Mission Trip." We counted nearly $400! Go Rita!

Privileged to be part of this quiet farm community, we enjoyed working with fully altruistic people.

CHAPTER 15

Turning 90

BIRTHDAYS PARTIES ARE DISTORTED. It seems like the older someone gets, the bigger the celebration should be. But the irony of that is that human energy levels never match the rising numbers! I would like to have put on a gala affair for Spurgeon on his 90th birthday. I wanted to truly honor his well-lived life but could never have matched or outdone his seventieth birthday party attended by 137 people from all over the United States and world! Moreover, I didn't have the energy to do it again twenty years later.

So, instead, I gave him a card party. My goal was to get ninety greetings, or more. I started months ahead, asking family to put it on their Facebook pages. Shucks, I felt no shame in suggesting that if there were four people in the family, each of them was welcome to send a card!

When May came, the mailman said, "Wow! Your husband is a popular guy! I have never delivered this many cards to a person in one day." He declared that on that day thirty-six cards were stuffed in our mailbox!

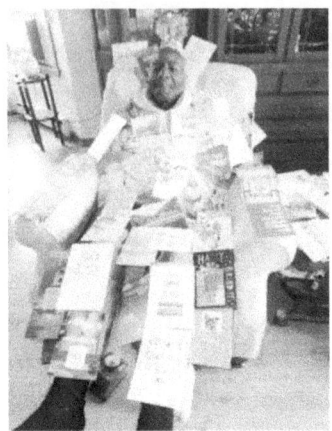

Spurgie and his 163 cards on his 90th birthday

It was fun to see the cards roll in over a couple weeks' time. Once it became evident to Spurgeon that we were going to get a big number, he started a daily count. And so did friends and family on Facebook. A common question became, "So what is the tally now?"

Early in the incoming collection, one of our eight-year-old church kids spilled the beans. He wrote in his card that I had asked the church to send cards so that's why he was complying. Adorable. So daily, for weeks, the loved Spurgeon Wiggins Jr. was lavished with sentiments of appreciation and admiration.

By the time all the stragglers came in, their sum was 163 cards.

We were particularly touched when a couple of young men and women we'd known since they were toddlers wrote letters stating how influential Spurgeon had been in their lives. These young people of God went on to be missionaries and pastors!

We had songs and a cake for the fitting occasion, too. Spurgeon was touched by a number of drop-ins, especially when his kid brother, William (who shares Spurgie's birth date, but was born seventeen years after Big Brother,) made a surprise visit to share the momentous day. We were grateful William found his way to our place, as he is a Vietnam vet drastically affected by exposure to Agent Orange.

It wasn't the party of a lifetime, but with presence, tenderness and hugs, he spent his final birthday.

The past year had been in slow motion. Our tradition was to dance the New Year away with Nat King Cole romance. After two songs, with a pained look on his face, we retreated to the love seat to do our "old year out, new year in" love discussion.

We'd also had problems with his food and water intake the whole previous year. It was like pulling teeth to get him to eat or drink, because he consistently insisted he was full. Little did we know that non-alcoholic cirrhosis of the liver was bloating him, quickly robbing him of his appetite and health. A simple blood test could have detected this disease, which kills many Americans each year. But his general practitioner failed to identify it. We didn't find out until three weeks prior to his death.

Here, again, Spurgeon's selflessness is worth telling about:

Our girlfriend and head librarian, Jennifer, told us of a historic resort in Northern Michigan, a restored Civilian Conservation Corp camp. Given that my bio father worked in the C.C.C, I was anxious to spend time at this retreat. They have a wonderful reputation for serving local produce at their planned meals, and we thought it would be lovely for someone else to cook for us for a week. Spurgeon made reservations for late July. Intending to take me there for my birthday, he found the resort to be full, so we went a couple of weeks early.

Our friend Mary, who attended a card club with Spurgeon each week at the local Council on Aging, said Spurgeon mentioned several times that he was elated to take me to this historic spot for a week of rest and relaxation. Here he was, weeks from his termination, and he was focusing on *my* happiness.

It is bewildering to me that I didn't catch his symptoms. Both my biological mom and brother, Wayne, died of liver disorders. I'd been fighting a challenged liver as long as I could remember. But when my liver is bad it very obvious: my skin feels like a garbage dump and itches like crazy and the eliminations of my body turn colorless. Beware, people, if your pee has no color: That means the liver is not removing the toxins from your blood like it is supposed to, because of illness. Same is true of pale (even white) feces.

However, these symptoms did not show up on Spurgeon, so we were left wondering why he had such a tremendous loss of thirst and appetite. Spurgeon and I wondered until it was too late. The nurse asked us, on Spurgie's third visit to the hospital in three weeks, if anyone had told us the real deal on his health status. Fearing her response, we said no.

"He has advanced cirrhosis of the liver and has a week to a month to live." So said Nurse Ratched.

As her heavy words rooted themselves in our hearts and minds, we looked at each other, not believing a word she said. This darling man's life-long goal was to live to be a hundred. The news did not fit the plan.

God had always seen Spurgeon through his health encounters. He had a double bypass at age sixty-nine, including the widow maker, but was out hunting deer in our forest one month later. He had prostate cancer on a grand scale, but God healed him completely without surgery. He lived with a pacemaker. At eighty-two years old he had brain surgery on his pituitary and was released thirty-six hours later with flying colors. Surely God would favor His honored son, Spurgeon, with the beauty of life one more time.

But then, He let His "only begotten Son" die for the universal good of mankind.

Spurgeon told me, "Take me home. I want to go home."

We had crossed many a faith bridge in our nearly forty years of marriage. We prayed in His will, once again, to let His favor shine on Spurgeon and save him from his body.

God chose to do just that by gifting him the beginning of everlasting life with a new body.

Five days after Spurgeon came home by ambulance, he passed to the other side. I'm guessing that his buddy, Harold, was the first to greet him.

CHAPTER 16

In Weakness There is Strength

I HAVE BEEN A person of strong emotion and exuberance all of my life. But when tragedy or trauma strikes, my M.O. is stoicism. It is evidently the way my body has figured out how to deal with severities. I warned the kids of my life-long approach to death, so they understood my behavior. Spurgeon's passing fried my brain.

That altered state of mind forced my thoughts to withdraw to the wrenching pain of my sophomore year in college, when the most significant love in my life died in Vietnam. My wonderful Uncle Al had perished in an attack on his Army compound. He had been my security blanket and my human love line to stability. We had written letters back and forth, sent cassette tapes to each other with voice messages. I'd sent him cookies at Christmas in a coffee can, just as Mom Hildur had done. And then, at my fragile age of nineteen, he was gone. His death put me in a zone that challenged my capacity to move forward, both then and now.

At this moment, with Spurgeon's passing, my whole body sensed that big changes were happening. I couldn't look at, nor be around food. If compelled to be near edibles, a gag reflex kicked in. I forgot to drink, got dehydrated and other unmentionable things. Weeks of unconscious fasting passed before I could get anything into my tummy.

I dropped thirty-eight pounds in four weeks. That had never been my experience.

Anger with God doesn't do it for me. Spurgeon and I often conversed about that very concept and agreed that it didn't make sense to blame the only One who is perfectly innocent. It *really* doesn't make sense to do what I have witnessed many times: On one hand people state they don't believe in God and the next minute that same person is blaming Him for the death of their father or the disease that had made them lame or another inequity of the hand they had been dealt. That God has the ability to stop illness in a fallen world does not make Him the bad guy if He doesn't. (Especially if we consider the rewards of His Kingdom.) Maybe He wants His favorite people near Him. I wouldn't fault anyone for that.

Initially, however, I was extremely angry that his doctor had not caught this common malady earlier. Fortunately for that doctor and my soul, I also adamantly believed that a man or women living in the center of God's will is absolutely invincible until the day that God calls him or her home.

Oddly enough, we did not discuss his dying in the time he spent doing just that. We talked about his immediate needs and his comfort, if we talked at all. He was in a perpetual state of fatigue and discomfort, so most of the time he preferred to lie quietly, no distractions.

Spurgeon, the wannabe centurion.

Two of our four children were able to come to his bedside, the other two were both dealing with spousal deaths. It was a stressful time for much of our family.

I saw the evidence. He was going to slip into a space that was between life and death. (I had witnessed deaths previously.) Just before that happened, Spurgeon looked deeply into my eyes and, as he loosely held my hand in his, spoke these tender words: "You are a wonderful wife."

He said that with a gentle smile and gifted me his sparkling eyes. His indomitable Spirit amazed me.

It intrigued me that he used the present tense. He didn't say, "You have been a wonderful wife."

I wondered if it was because he held out hope of a miracle to the very end. He spoke only in the present.

Staring into the face of my wannabe centurion, I knew if I responded from my heart's compulsion, there would be gushing tears and wailing. Little did he need that.

My only response was whispered, with a sigh of gratefulness, as his beautiful name seeped from my heart unto my lips and spilled into the air, along with the melody of his name. "Spurgeon . . ."

How typical of my beautiful man of God, that his last coherent words were those of encouragement. What a love. What a man.

Fortunately, our friends, Roger and Tanya, knew the ropes of death and stepped in to help guide us through those difficult decisions. And *all* decisions at this point are difficult.

Family and friends from all around the nation put their steps in order to make Spurgeon's going home a service to be remembered. My three brothers with whom I was raised, Mike, Bob, and Dave, called frequently to bolster me. Our favorite pastors and friends, Sam and Pam, came from Florida to officiate the memorial. Despite raging COVID-19, people flocked to help and reflect on the life of this stellar man of God.

All the happenings that make up a funeral were a blur to me. God implemented my autopilot mode. I don't know that I handled the proceedings well. I do know that my friends helped me and they handled it all very lovingly. I was in a daze.

Mind altering meds were out of the question, because I read an article that warned against them in circumstances of grief. Medicating your mind only delays the ultimate pain that your whole body, heart and soul, *must* deal with.

I couldn't imagine anything that would subdue the sorrow in my heart. The most magical creature in my life had gone to meet his reward. This was a big, sudden, permanent change, a bit like an avalanche on the side of a steep mountain.

There weren't too many thoughts in my head at the time, but an old thought emerged. Years ago, I bought a superb, name-brand greeting card. It pictured a round porch table with lace, two cups of tea, flowers and a verse that went something like this:

> "If I could sip tea with God, I would thank Him for lending you to me."

With all my being, that is the attitude I wanted to exhibit toward Spurgeon's home going. It is the attitude for which I prayed.

My gratitude for having Spurgeon as a husband all these wonderful years helped me find the truths that God needed me to know in this time of trial. The Wonderful Counselor and His Spirit had shown greater than the darkness that wanted to crush me. The Light impeded the darkness.

Perhaps most endearing of the many things God did for me happened at bedtime. For the first two weeks after Spurgeon's passing over, I experienced the weight of his arm around me and his chest warming my back as I fell asleep.

I know that sounds ridiculous, to some even morose, but that is precisely what happened.

Spurgeon and I adored sleeping together, and we fell asleep spooning each night. I wondered how I would drowse off without his arm around me. But each night, when I curled up in my spot, I felt the pressure of an arm embracing me and the warmth of a chest at my back. Initially, it alarmed me. But, quickly, it was too soothing to feel anything but loving comfort. I fell into deep sleep, embraced by Love.

When everyone left to resume their lives, I slept for days. Our bodies each have their own built-in pattern for healing. Twelve to fourteen hours of solid sleep was my norm for a month or so. It was nearly like I was in a form of hibernation, as when I slept, I logged zzzs straight through the night with no bathroom breaks and with zero consciousness of the time. Emotional fatigue engulfed me. Never had I slept like that. The few daytime hours remaining were dominated by the unending list of paperwork a widow/widower must wade through.

Then sleeplessness dominated. All the sleepy-time herbs and nighttime sleep aids on earth couldn't change that. Sadness, loneliness and sorrow walked hand in hand with me daily. A tremendous fear came over me, fear that I would live the rest of my life as half of a wheel, clumping along.

A half of a wheel clumping along for the remainder of life was not my idea of living. We had made such a wonderful impact as a team, working to resolve so many issues, all the while endeavoring to advance the cause of Christ. Now, alone, I felt totally incapable and insufficient.

Ah hah! That's it! *Fear*. I was enveloped in fright and didn't recognize it. Hadn't the lack of fear in my life been worn like a badge of honor?

I felt inadequate alone. I'd just spent thirty-seven years building up our marriage and now half of that enduring love was gone from earth forever. No amount of weeping or mourning would change that.

My own heart embarrassed me because I couldn't reconcile my faith with my feelings. I was in *The Word* daily and I believed every single one of God's promises about life hereafter, as I understood it. So why didn't I take that and run and act more like that competent woman of God that I used to be and that He wanted me to be?

I read in Ecclesiastes, shortly after Spurgeon went home, that it is better to sorrow than to glee, because you learn more sorrowing.

The stinging fact that I did not want to learn any more about grieving put a temporary roadblock to my progress. For once in my life, the teacher did not want to learn.

God knew my fears and sent one of our heart-girls, Janet, to move in for a number of months. She is half my age, hardworking, and needed a place to park while in-between jobs and apartments. She is also a good cook (she learned that from me) and made me eat and drink. Bossy little thing at times, too! But she got the job done. We did devotions together and prayed and spoke of outstanding Spurgie moments. We laughed and cried.

Then, the All Powerful Light pushed the deep shadows of fear back and I was reminded, through *The Word* in Ephesians (Chapter 1) that I have been given the Spirit of Wisdom and Revelation so that I might know Him better.

All I needed was radical trust. I am familiar with and have worked with that concept much of my life. I could do that.

My bio brother, Wayne, taught me unabated trust years ago at his family farm in Northern Minnesota. It was the summer before my junior year in college, and I spent a couple of weeks Up North with Wayne and family. While there, I was game to help with any job that my skills would meet.

Busy running a dozen tasks at a time, as farmers do, Wayne asked me to move the dump truck from the farm to the silos a couple miles away. There, Barb, his wife, would pick me up. I said that I would like to help in that manner, but I'd never driven a dump truck. My faith-filled brother said, "Well, you know how to drive a stick shift, right?"

"Of course," I stated adamantly.

"Then you can manage the truck. Just pay close attention to the gear-shift diagram painted on the stick. You can do it Deb. I believe in you," he stated affirmatively and walked away.

So, I drove the dump truck a couple of miles away and Barb picked me up. Didn't even grind hamburger on the way!

Then, my trusting brother asked me if I would run the combine for the afternoon.

"Wayne, really? That's a huge, expensive machine, and I don't want to hurt it!" I protested.

"Not to worry. I'll have Roy [our younger brother] show you how. He'll harvest several rows and turns with you, and then you can take over. It's very repetitive. You can do it, Deb. I believe in you," he stated in his calm voice, starting about his other business.

So, I drove the combine well into the evening, completing the day with mounting satisfaction. All because someone special believed I could do it.

And here was God, trusting me because He believed in me. The Master of the Universe took me by the hand and led me to think I could make something good out of the rest of my life, alone, with Him. He would show me how, and then I could work it.

It is an honor and a privilege to learn from Wisdom. I stopped resisting being the strong and capable woman I had been for years. His grace is sufficient for me.

Understanding enveloped me for the first time in my life in regard to that verse from 2 Corinthians 12:9 (NIV): "My grace is sufficient for you for my power is made perfect in weakness."

I never liked that verse because it was so inconvenient. I didn't want to think of myself as weak. A Viking woman from Minnesota, where they grow them strong and capable, does not pride herself in weakness.

But what was my fear really displaying here? Was it not the strong message that I needed to humble myself before God, recognizing that my former bravado was really a lack of humility?

Micah 6:8 (NIV) is outstandingly clear in that regard: "And what does the Lord require of you: but to do what is right, and love mercy and to walk humbly with your God." If that is not a clear enough message concerning humility, look up 2 Chronicles 7:14 and Psalms 25:9.

And what about "Perfect love casts out fear" (1 John 4:18, BLB). I began chanting a song by Josh Baldwin that encourages me to know that none of my phobias and trepidations can live on when I "Stand In Your Love."

I did believe every word of those truths. I just needed to be reminded. Besides that, I'd often been annoyed by people who pick and choose what they want to believe out of the Bible and leave the rest. I believe that C. S. Lewis was right when he wrote:

> I am trying here to prevent anyone saying the really foolish thing that people often say about Him, "I am ready to accept Jesus as a great moral teacher, but I don't accept his claim to be God." That is the one thing we must not say. A man who was merely a man and said the sort of things Jesus said would not be a great moral teacher. He would either be a lunatic—on a level with the man who says he is a poached egg—or else he would be the Devil of Hell. You must make your choice. Either this man was and is the Son of God; or else a madman or something worse. (Mere Christianity, Macmillan, 1952, pp. 55-56.)

And Jesus being real, then logic says the Bible follows the same rule: It's all or nothing. Either I believe in *The Word* in its entirety, or

I don't believe it at all. We don't have the right to choose what we like and/or agree with and toss out the rest for refuse. We don't know enough to pick and choose because we are not omniscient and can't see the big picture. It doesn't work like that.

"Where were you when I laid the foundation of the earth?" (Job 38:4, NLT)

Alas, giving in to the truth helped me get stronger. I capitulated in totality.

His grace *is* sufficient for me. With the truth in sight, decisiveness, and follow-through were now the keys to wellness.

Week after week, my Lord brought things to me that were lifesaving.

One day, while cleaning, I ran into six old love letters that Spurgie had written me. They were tender, precious, and heart-warming and brought a smile to my heart for days. I read them and reread them, held them to my chest, breathed on them, poured over them, kissed them, devoured them. I saw him beaming at me, as I read the tenderness and humor. Spurgeon's presence was so vivid.

This carried me over for weeks.

Some days after the found letters, my lack of tech awareness worked in my favor when I found out I had voice messages on my cell phone. My mobile phone is about a year old, and I know how to text messages but was unaware that it had a recorded voice mail.

And no, I am not writing this with a typewriter!

Amongst thirty other messages from miscellaneous people, I had three recordings from Spurgeon. Seeing that he had messages for me in his rich, loving voice drove me to complete ecstasy. I stared at them as if they were a vision. I pushed the button and the vision spoke!

They were each a paragraph long! I could relish everything from "Hey Babe" or "Hey *Amor*," to just hearing his love and concern.

It brought a smile to my heart to hear: "Hi Baby, It's your man. I just got home. I thought you'd beat me here. Wish you had your phone on. If you're not home soon I'm going to come looking for you. O.K., love you. See you soon."

My favorite message was exemplary of how precious our everyday words can be: "Hey *Amor*, Well, your dog came home. She looks tired and dirty and embarrassed. She won't even eyeball me. Anyway, I know you were worried about her. She's fine. I'm fine too, but I look forward to being together when you get home. Love you, Darling."

Everyday old stuff, right?

No, not really. This is the *great* stuff that makes relationships thrive! What wonderful anticipation this sets up for the speaker as well as the recipient. Joy follows the hearing as well as the reunion.

Even in death he impressed me.

That positivity helped me when grief came in unexpected waves. I would make headway in wellness, and then a huge, tidal wave of sadness washed over me, knocking me off my feet.

God persisted in sending kindnesses with each wave of grief, so that I would not be inundated.

I had a noon appointment to have blood drawn for a checkup. Since I had dutifully fasted from 6:00 the night before, I stopped at the grocery store and picked up something quick and nutritious before driving to a nearby park to consume my lunch. But on arrival, I had a complete breakdown as I pulled up to the scenic spot on Mill Pond. I turned off the engine, bowed my head, and let out the grief.

Having buried my head for some minutes, I sensed a shadow and presence at the driver's side window. Some minutes went by before I could lift my head with composure and see who the shadow was.

It turned out to be Shannon, one of Spurgeon's and my best fishing buddies. How many times had the three of us laughed and teased one another about the size of our fish or the "one that got away?" The two men seemed to have a father/son relationship.

Seeing Shannon waiting there reminded me of one gorgeous spring day when the three of us fished, and I struggled to pull in a whopper of a Northern Pike. The rod bent and the line swam back and forth in the lake, pulling and tugging. Ultimately the seasoned fish got away. Shannon had the audacity to tell me, "Eh, those were some healthy weeds you had there!"

I nearly pushed him into the lake at that moment!

And, now, that same, darling fishing buddy patiently waited while I painstakingly got myself together enough to respond to his presence.

Wiping my tears away, I rolled down the window, and we spoke of our wonderful, mutual friend, Spurgie. When I apologized for being such a mess and making him wait in the drizzle, he responded with words that salved my aching heart. "Deb, you are grieving in proportion to your investment. You are exactly where you are supposed to be."

Again, the loving words of a friend saved me from drowning in a tidal wave of grief and brought me to the truth, again: "Greater is He who is in you, than he who is in the world" (1 John 4:4, KJV).

My politically charged, feminist friend has followed the life of the admirable journalist Gloria Steinem, who married in her later years. Though I could not substantiate this via the internet, my astute friend said that Steinem stated that she finally found a "real man."

In my younger years, I would have wondered what she meant. There seemed to be a plentitude of men that qualified as a "real man." In my more discriminating years, having experienced a "real man," I not only felt what she meant but understood what must be done. Our men of God must submit themselves to His authority, (first the Jew and then to the Gentile, according to Romans 1:16) and be the leaders of the household and community the way they are meant to be. Our beds, homes, neighborhoods, cities and world would be vastly improved places to live.

Of course, what is good for the gander is also good for the goose and the following statement applies equally to all people. This is the resolve needed by everyone if we want to be told, "Well done, my good and faithful servant" (Matthew 25:21).

The brother of Jesus recognized that same need in the early church when he stated in James 4:17 (NLT), "Remember, it is sin to know what you ought to do and then not do it."

Way to go Spurgeon! You lived the life of a truly free man and the life of an overcomer, just like the book of Revelation describes.

John uses the word overcome eight times in the culminating book of *The Word*.

He writes things like this quote from the mouth of Christ: "Here on earth you will have many trials and sorrows. But take heart! I have overcome the world" (John 16:33, NLT).

I've always figured that was a bit audacious of God. (Don't worry. I know that He is omniscient, knows my every thought and is not offended by my explorative thinking.)

That He is infallible and we, fallible, He omnipotent and we, finite, does not dampen God's spirits in regard to His expectations of us. He insists on other seemingly rash statements like, "Be perfect, therefore, as your heavenly Father is perfect" (Matthew 5:48, NIV). That's a statement only He can make.

All of those expectations are daunting, are they not? But maybe, since we know we can't be perfect in everything, we can be perfect in the area that God has gifted us strength.

If giving is our spiritual gift, we can be perfect givers. If encouragement is our gift, we can be the most supportive individual known to friends and family. If we superbly manage a gift of hospitality throughout our lives, we can gift everyone who eats bread or drinks water at our house the love of God that dwells in us.

If we all make a concerted effort to use our greatest skills to express God's love to everyone we come in contact with, God will be honored, and we have done our best and pleased Him. What better thing than to cause the Maker to be happy? Spurgeon's resolve toward responsibilities was adopted from Edward Everett Hale's philosophy: "I am only one, but I am one. I cannot do everything, but I can do something. What I can do, I should do and, with the help of God, I will do!" (Federer, William Joseph, Federer, William J. America's God and Country: Encyclopedia of Quotations. United States: Fame, 1994, p. 271).

God turns around and says, "I'm sending you help, call on the Comforter." (Paraphrased from John 14:16). It's good to have that help.

Spurgeon overcame deep poverty, a sketchy education, stuttering, a cruel environment, a war, a failed marriage, the lure of the world, and institutional racism to become the premier man that God groomed him to be.

If he can do all that, and I lived with his stellar example for nearly forty years, then I can overcome also.

Uffda! A lot of work ahead!

CHAPTER 17

Interactive Fun Stuff

THIS IS AN INTERACTIVE chapter with fun items that have been referenced throughout the book. Pick and choose or run the gamut!

LOTS OF PHOTOS:

Our digital world is fascinating. There are seventy photos of Spurgeon's life in his memorial found at: brownfuneralhomeniles.com.

It features a recording of the tribute service, which should run on their site unendingly. Here's how: Log in the above site and go to obits and click on that. Enter Spurgeon's name in the search engine. When his site comes up, press on his photo to find all the pictures, the obit, as well as the entire service. Choose what you like.

The singer with the pure voice is our granddaughter, Janielle. The scripture reader is our sweet friend, Anna, 17 years old. The prayer is by her Daddy, Roger. Pastor Sam officiates.

MORE OF MY PERUVIAN ART:
Some previously published, some not, and more mission trip photos.

Lake Titicaca

Matchupitchu

Mississippi Meets Minnesota

Mission trip

Cruising the Amazon

OUR GUMBO RECIPE:

WIGGINS SEAFOOD GUMBO

1 cup bacon fat
1 cup all-purpose flour
10 stalks celery, chopped
3 large yellow onions, chopped
1 bunch green onions, chopped
1 green pepper, chopped
1/2 cup fresh chives, chopped
3 cloves garlic, minced
1/2 cup parsley, chopped
1 1/2 lb okra, sliced crosscut
2 1/2 tbsp. shortening
2 quarts chicken stock
2 quarts water
1/2 cup Worcestershire sauce
2 tbsp Tabasco sauce
1/2 cup catsup
(1) 16 oz. can whole tomatoes
1 ring bologna, crosscut thinly
1 large slice of ham, chopped
3 bay leaves
1/2 tsp thyme
1/2 tsp rosemary
2 cups cooked chicken, chopped
1 lb shelled crabmeat
4 pounds shrimp
Lemon juice to taste

Heat the bacon grease over medium heat, pouring in the flour little by little. Stir constantly until it turns a milk chocolate-like brown. (This takes a long time.) Meanwhile, you can cook off the bologna slices in a dry pan with no fat. Fry the okra slices in the shortening until slightly brown. Add to the brown roux (flour and grease) all of the vegetables and seasonings.

Cook this one hour on simmer, stirring frequently. Add the okra, bologna coins, water, ham, and tomatoes. Stir. Add the chicken, shrimp, and crab and simmer 30 minutes more just until the shrimp are lightly cooked. Add lemon juice. Pour over a hearty bowl of warm brown rice.

WORLD VISION GOAL:

The reader may recall that we are long-standing fans of the World Vision organization that has fed starving people of the world for seven decades. The reason for our long-standing dedication to this dynamic help organization is they use only 12 percent of the gifted monies for the administrative staff while 82 percent actually reaches the child you choose to support. With this in mind, Spurgeon and I decided long ago (when the cost of building a well in a foreign country of need was $7,000) that we would like to dig a well. The rise in cost resulted in an augmented sum of $15,000 per well. A substantial percentage of the profits of this book will go toward accomplishing that life-long desire.

SPONTANEOUSLY ROMANTIC:

I found this valentine amongst our memories. Spurgeon created it after ten to fifteen years of marriage. We were teaching Kids Club at our church and making Valentines, kids to parents. The poem is very intimate and sentimental, so I'm glad you can't read it all, but the opening is precious. He begins...

Spontaneously romantic

I am the sun,

You are the moon.

I am the song,

You are the tune.

You are the great Milky Way

And I am the one with the stars in his eye.

No wonder I was head over heels in love with this man!

RULES TO HAND AND FOOT:

These are the rules to one of the hottest table games across the nation, as is proven in campground social halls all over the United States.

HAND & FOOT

(4 Players-5 decks / 6 Players-7 decks)

Each player get 11 cards to start with called the HAND, plus 11 more called the FOOT

In order to LAY down, the
1st hand you need …….90 points   2nd "   "   "   ……120 points
3rd "   "   "   ……140 points   4th "   "   "   …….160 points

Jokers count…50 Points   Kings, Queens, Jacks, 10,
2's count……..20 Points   9, 8, count 10 Points each
A's count…….20 Points   7-6-5-4-3's Count 5 points each…
    EXCEPT RED "3" they count <u>500</u> **points off your score if you're caught holding one and someone goes out.**
Black(dirty) piles count 300 Points to the good & Red (Clean) piles count 500 Points to the good. You need 7 cards to make either a clean or dirty pile. You can't lay down 3's
You can have 1 wild card with 2 cards
    "   "   " 2 "   "   " 3 cards
    "   "   " 3 "   "   " 4 cards

YOU MAKE MY HEART FLUTTER:

Love letters from the past.

A photo of the wonderful love letters that made my heart swoon.

You make my heart flutter

OLE AND LENA JOKE

Here is a link to hear one of many infamous Ole and Lena Jokes: https://fb.watch/d-2TS58JRP/. On Facebook, search for Mississippi MEETS Minnesota.

A.T.V. MINISTRY IDEA, *WHEEL TO HEAL*: Above is also the link to a personal four-wheeling trip flick that our granddaughter, Brittany, arranged. The adventure took place on Drummond Island, Michigan, a true four-wheeling haven. To view the film, visit the site named above.

Drummond Island

One year after the passing of our beautiful Spurgeon, the lovely Brit came to visit me in Michigan from Arizona for the express purpose of an adventure on wheels. We left on this escapade with a loaded truck and trailer and two very heavy hearts. The more memories we shared about Spurgie, the more we flip-flopped from sad to sweet.

When we reached our destination, we unloaded the A.T.V.s and started rolling. The fresh air, wind in our hair, and newfound freedom of riding together began to erase the sadness. Each bump and mile of lush, wild Michigan eked out more adrenaline and positive moods. We bathed in the beauty of the Northern woods for a week, four-wheeling six to ten hours a day. The two sad sacks who had departed earlier returned home with stellar attitudes, ready again to face the rigors of life.

Given the above experience of healing, I am currently starting a ministry for oppressed or depressed women. I purchased a second, used four-wheeler, obtained one more helmet, am gathering a short list of men who will lend me their trailers, and studied to find the closest State O.R.V. and A.T.V. paths from my home.

Since the closest good courses are three-and-one-half hours from here, we will make it an overnight trip. I will prepare great healthy food, both spiritual and gastrointestinal. We will *Wheel to Heal* for two full days. Then return home.

If you would like to ask questions or make a comment about this book, please feel comfortable to do so on the business page named above.

I look forward to hearts looking to the Light and burdens being lifted.

Photo Credits

Pg 12 used with permission of author; personal album

Pg 17 used with permission of author; personal album

Pg 18 used with permission of author; personal album

Pg 27 top; used with permission of author; personal album

Pg 27 bottom; used with permission of author; personal album

Pg 28 used with permission of author; personal album

Pg 29 used with permission of author; personal album

Pg 30 used by permission of Powell Creative Services; Chicago, IL; 1981

Pg 41 used with permission of author; personal album

Pg 43 used with permission of author; personal album

Pg 47 used with permission of author; personal album

Pg 48 used with permission of author; personal album

Pg 60 used with permission of author; personal album

Pg 69 used with permission of author; personal album

Pg 72 top; used with permission of author; personal album

Pg 72 bottom; used with permission of author; personal album

Pg 74 used with permission of author; personal album

Pg 80 used with permission of author; personal album

Pg 98 used with permission of author; personal album

Pg 104 used with permission of author; personal album

Pg 106 used by permission of Jennifer Layne; Kelsey Lake Association, Cassopolis, MI; 2018

Pg 108 top; used by permission of author; personal album

Pg 108 bottom; used with permission of author; personal album

Pg 113 used with permission of author; personal album

Pg 116 used with permission of author; personal album

Pg 124 used with permission of author; personal album

Pg 140 top; used with permission of author; personal album

Pg 140 bottom; used with permission of author; personal album

Pg 141 top; used with permission of author; personal album

Pg 141 bottom; used with permission of author; personal album

Pg 143 used with permission of author; personal album

Pg 144 used with permission of author; personal album

Pg 145 top; used with permission of author; personal album

Pg 145 bottom; used with permission of author; personal album

Pg 149 used with permission of author; personal album

Front Cover: used with permission of author; personal album

Back Cover: used by permission of Jera Krager; Vandalia, MI; 2007

ABOUT THE AUTHOR

Like a love story forged in diversity, Mississippi Meets Minnesota takes readers on a journey exploring a life of creativity. Bohemian lifestyle teacher, artist, traveler and long-time lover of God, Deb Wiggins lays out how she and her husband, went about seeking a lifestyle centered on giving, and found a life filled with abundance.

www.ingramcontent.com/pod-product-compliance
Lightning Source LLC
LaVergne TN
LVHW091300080426
835510LV00007B/335